Cambridge Elements

Elements in the History of Philosophy and Theology in the West
edited by
Alexander J. B. Hampton
University of Toronto

POPPER, PHILOSOPHY AND FAITH

Anthony O'Hear
University of Buckingham

Shaftesbury Road, Cambridge CB2 8EA, United Kingdom

One Liberty Plaza, 20th Floor, New York, NY 10006, USA

477 Williamstown Road, Port Melbourne, VIC 3207, Australia

314–321, 3rd Floor, Plot 3, Splendor Forum, Jasola District Centre, New Delhi – 110025, India

103 Penang Road, #05–06/07, Visioncrest Commercial, Singapore 238467

Cambridge University Press is part of Cambridge University Press & Assessment, a department of the University of Cambridge.

We share the University's mission to contribute to society through the pursuit of education, learning and research at the highest international levels of excellence.

www.cambridge.org
Information on this title: www.cambridge.org/9781009626798

DOI: 10.1017/9781009626811

© Anthony O'Hear 2025

This publication is in copyright. Subject to statutory exception and to the provisions of relevant collective licensing agreements, no reproduction of any part may take place without the written permission of Cambridge University Press & Assessment.

When citing this work, please include a reference to the DOI 10.1017/9781009626811

First published 2025

A catalogue record for this publication is available from the British Library

ISBN 978-1-009-62679-8 Hardback
ISBN 978-1-009-62678-1 Paperback
ISSN 3033-3954 (online)
ISSN 3033-3946 (print)

Cambridge University Press & Assessment has no responsibility for the persistence or accuracy of URLs for external or third-party internet websites referred to in this publication and does not guarantee that any content on such websites is, or will remain, accurate or appropriate.

For EU product safety concerns, contact us at Calle de José Abascal, 56, 1°, 28003 Madrid, Spain, or email eugpsr@cambridge.org

Popper, Philosophy and Faith

Elements in the History of Philosophy and Theology in the West

DOI: 10.1017/9781009626811
First published online: May 2025

Anthony O'Hear
University of Buckingham

Author for correspondence: Anthony O'Hear, anthony@ohear.com

Abstract: This Element aims to make good an imbalance in scholarly work on the thought of Karl Popper. Towards the end of his life he developed a dualistic view of the self, and connected to it, a model of reality consisting of three worlds: first the inorganic world; a second level domain of consciousness; and a third world of ideas, institutions and concepts. This third world develops beyond the ideas and understanding of its human inventors. The implications of these later developments have not been fully considered, nor has his idea that his critical rationalism rests on an irrational faith. These are considered against the context of his more famous work on science and the open society. Popper saw his late work in quasi-Platonic terms, and the similarities and differences here are explored. Does Popper's work as a whole tend in an unfulfiled Platonic direction or need a religious foundation?

Keywords: Popper, self, world 3, Platonism, irrational faith

© Anthony O'Hear 2025

ISBNs: 9781009626798 (HB), 9781009626781 (PB), 9781009626811 (OC)
ISSNs: 3033-3954 (online), 3033-3946 (print)

Contents

1 Introduction — 1

2 Philosophy of Science: Conjectures and Refutations — 4

3 Social and Political Philosophy — 21

4 Popper's Later Philosophy: The Self and the Three Worlds — 38

5 Conclusion: Popper's Vision — 57

References — 62

1 Introduction

1.1 Life and Career

Sir Karl Raimund Popper CH, FRS, FBA, was born in Vienna in 1902 and died in Kenley, Surrey in 1994. For the latter part of his life, from 1946 onwards, he lived in England and was closely associated with the London School of Economics, where he nurtured and led a distinguished philosophy department, devoted particularly to the study of science and its philosophy. He was rightly honoured for his achievements in Britain, but also in many other countries too. He was unusual among his philosophical contemporaries in being widely read and admired by people outside the philosophical academy, by distinguished scientists and also by distinguished politicians, including the leaders of a number of countries. These included Mario Soares of Portugal, Helmut Kohl of Germany and Vaclav Havel of Czechoslovakia (as it then was). But, from 1937 before he took up what turned out to be permanent residence in England, he had spent eight years in New Zealand.

For the first part of his life Popper had lived and worked in Vienna. His father was a distinguished lawyer and his mother was an accomplished musician. Both had renounced their Judaism, and had officially converted to Lutheranism; this somewhat notional Lutheranism made little impact on Popper himself at any stage of his life. Nevertheless, from a very early age he was impressed and sickened by the abject poverty he saw around him in the Vienna of the time. As he remarked much later 'few people now living in the Western democracies know what poverty meant at the beginning of this (i.e. 20th) century'.[1] He also greatly admired the exploits of the Norwegian explorer and philanthropist Fridtjof Nansen. This early humanitarianism and love of exploration (and mountains) stayed with him for the rest of his life.

While in Vienna in the 1920s and 1930s Popper associated with many of that city's leading philosophers, musicians and intellectuals, who themselves had worldwide influence. But this did not mean that Popper followed any of them, either in whole or in part. Many of these intellectuals were followers of Marx or Freud or both, and some doctrinaire scientific materialists as well. In short they showed strongly anti-religious and atheistical prejudices, but while not uncritical of religious dogmatism, Popper was never entirely hostile to religious in general, nor was he an atheist. Two of Popper's major ideological battles were against the atheistical Marx and Freud. As time went on he became hostile to materialist accounts of human nature, while his attitude to religion was always

---

[1] Popper (1992), 9.

one of respectful agnosticism. Or, was it something closer to an actual religious attitude, if not embracing any sectarian faith?

In a short interview conducted in 1969 by Rabbi Edward Zerin, Popper professes agnosticism about the existence of God, but he also rejects dogmatic atheism as 'arrogant and ignorant'. We should admit that we don't know, and continue to search. He goes on to say 'I do think that all men, including myself, are religious. We all believe in something more important ... than ourselves ... a Third World, something which is beyond us and with which we do interact ... and through which we can transcend ourselves'.[2] What he means by the Third World we will see later, but for the moment we can simply note that it is quite possible to see Popper's philosophy of science, and his faith in it as an unending quest in terms of a quasi-religious self-transcendence, even though, as we will argue in the conclusion to this Element, his sense of religious is idiosyncratic. When we look at his account of science, however, it is clear that from the start Popper's thought was very different from the materialistic positivism of his Viennese contemporaries.

But, as is well known by the mid-1930s life in Austria became impossible for people of Jewish descent, even if, like Popper, they were thoroughly assimilated (and, in Popper's case, anti-Zionist to boot). So, when in 1937 he was offered a post in the University of Canterbury in Christchurch New Zealand, he accepted. All three periods in Popper's life – Vienna, New Zealand, London – were significant for his philosophical development and reputation.

Popper's reputation today rests largely on his work in two areas of philosophy, the philosophy of science and political philosophy. In both he made major contributions, and his influence will undoubtedly feature prominently in any future history of philosophy and thought more generally. In this essay I will say something about the reasons for this, which I believe are well merited. I will also show that his views about science and society were from the start somewhat outside the thinking current at the time, though this is not always fully appreciated. But, my main aim in this essay will be to show that it would be wrong to characterize Popper as primarily a specialist thinker in either the philosophy of science or in political thought. His vision is much wider than that, as becomes clear in looking at his work from the late 1960s onwards.

In this late work he offers a strikingly dualistic account of the self and what he called 'its' brain, with the brain open to impulses from the self. It also argued for what he dubbed a 'third' world of ideas and institutions above and beyond its embodiments in this world, but influencing both the 'second' world of human consciousness, and through us the material 'first' world. What is strange is that

---

[2] Zerin (1998), 47–8; quoted in Hacohen (2000), 68–9.

this material seems not to have provoked anything like the attention of his work in the philosophy of science or politics. Indeed in Vienna in 2002 there was a major celebration of the centenary of Popper's birth, at which there were more than 250 lectures and papers. Of these only two were on his three worlds thesis and none at all on his radically Cartesian view of the self. I hope in this essay in a small way to remedy this lacuna. His later work is as worthy of study and attention as the earlier, and he also helps us to understand the context in which that earlier work should be seen.

1.2 Two Formative Moments: 1919

Popper was clearly a precocious young man, because two moments in 1919, before his seventeenth birthday, profoundly influenced the thinking for which he was later to become renowned throughout the world. The first of these moments was in the May of that year, when the observations made by Eddington in the Atlantic Ocean to observe a total eclipse of the sun were taken to show that Einstein's theory of gravity was correct where Newton's was wrong. In other words, these observations constituted a deciding test between Einstein and Newton; Newton's theory, for all the two centuries or more of its observational confirmation and dominance in so broad a scientific field was wrong. For Popper this was absolutely compelling. Even the most successful scientific theory (most successful ever, in this case) is liable eventually to be shown to be wrong and to be replaced by a better challenger. We will examine the implications of all this for Popper's mature philosophy of science in the next section.

The second event of 1919 that was seminal for Popper's thinking was in the June of that year. An attempted communist coup in Vienna led to government soldiers firing on and killing a number of people in a crowd that was besieging the Horlgasse police station. Popper himself was in that crowd, and clearly sympathetic to its aims. Indeed he said that at that time for two or three months he had regarded himself as a communist. However, he became completely disenchanted with the whole communistic project when he saw that its leaders actually welcomed the loss of life of their own supporters on the grounds that the police brutality which had occurred then would allow them to whip up further revolutionary fervour and so hasten the onset of a proletarian regime. This was wholly unacceptable to the young Popper for three reasons. First, the loss of life was not anything to be welcomed or used. Secondly, the intellectuals behind the uprising and making use of the horror of the police shooting had no right to claim to represent the proletariat. And thirdly, neither these intellectual leaders nor anyone else could know the future for which they were so happy to sacrifice life. As Popper put it later in *Unended Quest*, his intellectual autobiography, 'it was a terrible thing to arrogate to oneself a kind of knowledge which made it a duty to risk the lives other people for an uncritically accepted dogma, for a dream that might turn out not to be realizable'.[3]

2 Philosophy of Science: Conjectures and Refutations

From the late 1920s, after a flirtation first with pedagogy and then with psychology, and also a certain amount of practical carpentry, Popper began to move into epistemology and the philosophy of science. Vienna was the home of the so-called 'Vienna Circle' of largely materialistically inclined logicians and philosophers of science. This group, which included such well-known names as Rudolf Carnap, Herbert Feigl and Otto Neurath, took their lead from Wittgenstein's *Tractatus Logic-Philosophicus*, whose ostensible purpose was to demarcate meaningful from meaningless forms of speech. Part of the motivation in this was a desire to cleanse language and thought of empty pseudo-profundity and to rid culture of unenlightened religion and obscurantist metaphysics, all of which were in line with the similar slate-clearing trends of the time in music, in the visual arts and in architecture.

Wittgenstein himself was personally out of sympathy with the hard-line scientism of the Vienna Circle, the attitude that science was to be regarded as the touchstone of good sense and practice. Nevertheless in proposition 6.53 of the *Tractatus* he said that 'whenever someone ... wanted to say something metaphysical ... he had failed to give a meaning to certain signs in his propositions'.[4] What he was saying was meaningless, in other words. This was the spirit behind the famous verifiability principle of the Circle: a proposition is meaningful if and only if it is either a proposition of logic or mathematics (and so true by virtue of meaning), or it is empirically verifiable. The verification principle had to be modified owing to certain quickly discovered difficulties, including the obvious one that the principle itself is neither true by virtue of meaning nor empirically verifiable. Nevertheless, its spirit in various modified forms continues to dominate academic philosophy in the Anglo-American world. Science, logic and mathematics, if not the only domains of meaningful discourse, are the touchstones of truth, from which all other forms of discourse and practice fall short.

Popper's early masterpiece, *The Logic of Scientific Discovery*, appeared in German in 1934 and was well received within the Vienna Circle.[5] However, as he was later to emphasize, he was never a member of the Circle. His book was different in spirit from that of the Circle and the verification principle. First, in it,

---

[3] Popper (1992), 34.   [4] Wittgenstein (1961), 6.53.   [5] Popper (1959).

he was not proposing a theory of meaning (and he was in fact always hostile to what he called meaning analysis). In Popper's view (and in Wittgenstein's later view) plenty of meaningful sentences would fall foul of the verification principle, including metaphysical statements, such as the tantalizing and intellectually fruitful pre-Socratic claims that 'everything changes' or that 'the world consists of atoms and the void'. Indeed, in Popper's view many of the most admired scientific theories have metaphysical statements of this sort as their inspiration; thus the widely held pre-Newtonian view that there is no physical action at a distance, adherence to which caused Newton himself considerable grief over gravity, which in his system amounts to action at a distance. But while not proposing a criterion of the meaning of any sort, Popper does propose a criterion to demarcate between scientific statements and non-scientific ones. According to this criterion, a scientific theory or statement must be empirically falsifiable. And here we touch on the second major difference between Popper and the Vienna Circle philosophers.

To see this, remember first the Eddington observations, taken by Popper to falsify the Newtonian system. What made, or appeared to make, this event so decisive was the logic of the situation. The Newtonian system consisted of general or universal statements, such as for every action there is an equal and opposite reaction. Note, every, which means at all times and places. But we cannot observe all times and places, particularly not those in the future, those in the remote past and those throughout the universe which are spatially distant from us. So, if all times and places include myriads of events we cannot observe, we cannot verify a law or theory such as Newton's. We cannot show it to be *true*, which is what 'verify' means. We might observe many events which are in accord with it, but there will be countless others we cannot observe. How do we know that they will all follow the patterns we had observed up to now and in our little segment of space? So verification of a universal scientific theory is beyond us, which is another problem with the verification principle beyond its own unverifiability. What the Vienna Circle took to be the model of meaningfulness and rationality – scientific theorizing – consisted crucially of unverifiable statements, the laws and theories of science itself, on which so much of the modern world and its prestige rested.

At this point many people, including many philosophers and scientists will invoke what is called a or the principle of induction. That is, they will say that when we have a lot of experience in a certain area, and it all goes one way, we are then entitled to assume, inductively it would be said, that the future will carry on in the same way. After all, we know that placing a steel bridge over a river will, in specified circumstances, provide a safe way of crossing the river. Negatively, we also know from experience that jumping from a high building will damage or kill anyone who tries it. In both cases, experience from the past is taken, correctly enough, to be a good guide to the future. And if someone asks why we should take past experience to be a good guide to the future, we can surely reply that acting in this way – relying on past experience, and learning from experience – has served us well in the past, and rather better than if we had chosen to ignore past experience.

Although not strictly identical with inductive inference (i.e. generalizing from masses of past experiences and observations), closely connected to it, at least since the time of Francis Bacon in the early seventeenth century, is the idea that good science should proceed from making observations uncontaminated by theory, expectations or prejudice. Bacon formulated a highly influential account of science along these lines, attempting in this way to explain the exponential growth of science since the mid sixteenth century, as freed from the prejudices and presuppositions of earlier science, dominated as it was by Aristotelian theory. The scientific revolution had occurred because, for the first time scientists simply observed, without theory or preconception.

But according to Popper this is quite wrong, both about the growth of science and, more precisely, about how observation should be conceived. Popper is insistent, rightly insistent indeed, that no observation can ever be without some idea of which particular segment of one's environment or angle on it one is focusing on. The exhortation to 'observe', and even more the instruction to observe everything in one's surroundings are both empty and unfulfillable. They are empty because they don't tell us what or what sort of thing we should be looking at or for. They are unfulfillable because the idea that one should observe and record everything that is surrounding one is no more fulfillable than was Tristram Shandy's ever-receding quest to record everything that had happened to him from his infancy. In both cases we will need a criterion of selection, some idea of what sort of thing we should be looking at or which aspects of one's life one should be recording. So, for Popper the Baconian idea, still held by many today, that science should proceed by means of presuppositionless observation is a fallacy.

It is, though, a fallacy often connected with theorists of science, such as Bacon, who want to be seen as firmly empiricist in the sense that they are sticking to the facts, and conducting their research without being influenced by theories. They should collect and collate their observations, and only then draw theoretical conclusions from their data. For Popper this is also incorrect. Far from being based on presuppositionless observation, as Bacon and his followers would have it, scientific research should be seen as an attempt to solve or answer problems thrown up within and by some theoretical framework. It is work guided by theory and directed to problems which arise from the theory or theories in which one is working. This is how science has found a focus since the scientific revolution which Bacon misinterpreted as being a matter of the collection of preuppositionless data. It is in critically addressing problems within a theoretical framework that science has been so fruitful over the past several centuries.

As well as demolishing a popular view of how science progresses, from the start Popper found what he saw as crucial problems in inductive reasoning more precisely. First, following the sceptical David Hume, he pointed out that there is a fatal circularity in the reasoning sketched two paragraphs ago, to the effect that having made our observations in the past we are justified in relying on what they tell us in the future. The inductivist says that we are entitled to rely on past experience (i.e. rely on inductive argumentation) because doing so has served us well in the past. Bridges hold up, leapers from high buildings come to grief. But in appealing to past experience to justify our relying on past experience now are we not assuming just what we are trying to prove? We are using past experience of apparently inductive success to justify our relying on inductive reasoning now. The whole defence is fatally circular and can carry no conviction.

But, apart from the manifest circularity involved in defending induction inductively, are we safe to think that past experience does in fact show that the future is always going to be like the past? Or, more pointedly, is it the case that even our most highly confirmed theories will always turn out to be confirmed? That they are liable not to be is just what Eddington's observations showed. Newton's theory, perhaps the most successful scientific theory ever, turned out in the end to be false. One of its implications, which Eddington was testing, turned out not to be as Newton's laws predicted; but it did turn out to be in conformity with the rival (Einstein's) theory. So, it seemed, more than two centuries of scientific success was turned on its head. And we can also think of more commonplace refutations of previous examples of inductive reasoning, such as the discovery that there was a mid-night sun (in the Arctic) or that bread can kill as well as nourish (ergotism), to take two of Popper's own examples.[6]

However, from Popper's point of view, all was not lost. For the very thing that seemed to be the scientific Achilles heel turns out to be its logical and methodological strong point. We cannot verify a scientific theory, but we can show it to be false, and do so definitively. A universal theory has countless implications, over the whole of space and time, and even if we can confirm a good number of them, myriads more will escape our scrutiny, and so verification or confirmation will always be at best partial and liable to mislead, as in the Newton–Einstein case. But, by pure logic, the falsification of a universal theory needs just one

---

[6] See Popper (1978), 10–11.

counter-instance. That all swans were white had seemed to be universally confirmed until one black swan was observed. One black swan shows that not all swans are white, for however long we had observed only white swans. Logically we cannot verify (show true) a universal theory because of its countless consequences, but by pure logic, we can falsify a universal theory with just one of its consequences being a counter-example.

So, Popper's key point in *The Logic of Scientific Discovery* and indeed in his subsequent philosophy of science is that the strength and virtue of the scientific method is that it allows us to falsify theories, and to do so with logical compulsion. If only one implication of a scientific theory is shown to be false, then the theory is falsified or, in his terms, refuted. (Please note that Popper uses the term 'refute' correctly, to mean that some claim is shown to be false, and not just that someone rejects it.) Going on from this, Popper sees the key criterion of a scientific theory is that it has refutable or falsifiable implications, either immediately or through a chain of inferences (as was the case in the observations made by Eddington). What scientists should do is to specify as strongly as they can what the implications of their favoured theory might be, and then go on to test them through observation and experiment. If the theory survives a severe test, well and good; work with it for the time being; but go on to look into other implications, until, as happens to most of the theories we have known about in the past, it comes up against a falsifying instance.

This last point has recently been dubbed by some philosophers of science the pessimistic meta-induction, that is, as past experience has shown that most, if not all, of the one-time leading scientific theories have proved to be false and have been replaced by a better one, it is likely that even our best theories will in the future suffer the same fate. Popper would not like talk of induction here, but he would certainly approve of the spirit. Indeed he continually emphasizes that scientific explanations are never complete or basic. They will always leave problems unsolved, as well as resting on basic theories which themselves stand in need of further explanation, and even if *per impossibile* we hit on the last, absolutely basic theory (Hawkins' mythical and somewhat hubristic 'theory of everything'), we would still not know why things ended there, just like that, as a brute inexplicable fact. But, as Popper himself points out, we are very far from having reached any ultimate explanation. Quantum theory, he continually urged, is 'clearly incomplete … it cannot be said to have led to prediction or explanation of the many new elementary particles which have been found in recent years'. Popper wrote this in 1977.[7] If anything the situation is even more bewildering in the third decade of the twenty-first century, with talk of

---

[7] Popper and Eccles (1977), 61–2.

antimatter so as to balance equations and the very strange behaviour of many of the entities postulated in modern physics, neither waves nor particles, it seems, but exercising puzzling powers of influencing other entities at speeds beyond that of light, to say nothing of the countlessly many worlds some will invoke to account for apparent randomness in this world, or of the ever elusive unification of relativity and quantum theory.

It is important to stress once again that Popper's falsification (or criterion of demarcation, as he calls it) is not a theory of meaning. It is an attempt to demarcate between scientific theories and other theories and ideas. As we have already seen, Popper welcomes untestable metaphysical claims into the scientific arena, as inspiring scientific enquiry and research, but, to become properly scientific, empirically testable implications have to be drawn from them in the form of universal theories with observable implications, which would specify just where they might be refuted. (Thus, if our theory says that every action had an equal and opposite reaction, we will know that it implies that the next time I push a door with a certain force, there will be a physical reaction of an equal force – a testable and measurable implication, in other words.) One might wonder why testability, beyond being an inspiring idea, is so important for Popper. The answer is that scientific testability is a key example of what he generalizes as the critical approach.

In Popper's view, the critical approach had already been present in the way the pre-Socratic philosophers from the sixth century BC had criticized and attempted to answer each other's speculations, and this critical spirit was something new in world history, a point we shall return to in the next section. However, it was only with the Scientific Revolution of the sixteenth and seventeenth centuries that the critical spirit took on an empirical edge, testing scientific theories against hard factual evidence, which is what Bacon was trying to explain in his misguided way by taking presuppositionless observation to be the key. For Bacon scientists in the Middle Ages erred in following Aristotelian dogma without question. For Popper, by contrast, the key was not presuppositionless observation, but the critical testing of theories against empirical observation and experiment. This was not only a major positive innovation in human culture, it was also what underlay the dramatic progress in the empirical sciences thenceforward.

So, for Popper and for many others, the accolade of a view or theory being scientific was prestigious. It came to be seen as the defining characteristic of human progress within the last half millennium, visible, tangible progress, as both science and the associated technologies began to play an increasingly important and often beneficial role in the lives of everyone on the planet. Of course, there were regrettable effects of this phenomenon as well, such as the development of atomic weaponry and the spoliation of many natural habitats, but in the main, these did little to diminish the prestige in which science has been and still is held, which takes us to the significance of Popper's criterion of demarcation between science and non-science. For it suggests, and certainly suggested to Popper, that the claim of two of the most significant currents of thought over the past century or more to be scientific are in fact bogus.

Both of these currents of thought had been influential in the Vienna of the 1920s, and Popper had certainly been involved in the relevant movements and discussions, to some extent favourably. The currents were Freudianism, and psychoanalysis more generally, and Marxism. They each fell short of scientific standing, but for a different reason. Insisting that a scientific theory had to make testable and potentially falsifiable predictions, Popper argued that psychoanalysis and analysists such as Freud and Adler (Viennese both) failed at the first scientific hurdle. Their theories failed to make any potentially falsifiable predictions. Any behaviour on the part of a patient, whether she loved or hated her father or he loved or hated his mother, could be brought within the generous parameters of a psychological analysis, and explained in its terms. So the theories, such as they were, with all their apparatus of unconscious psychic forces and subconscious drives and motivations undetectable except through analysis, were not scientific. In pressing this point Popper may have done damage to psycho-analytical practice, to the extent that it rests on pretensions to scientific status and validity. But it should be pointed out that Popper himself was never completely hostile to the ideas of Freud and the others. He felt that they could often throw light on the behaviour of individual agents, and he never intended to deny that we are all subject to ill-understood emotions and unrecognized motivations, which could be brought to light. The understanding offered by psychoanalysis, to the extent that it was valid was more like the insights afforded by literature and drama, from where indeed many of its revealing but unscientific insights stemmed.

Marxism was the second and in some ways more significant of Popper's 'unscientific' targets, more significant not just because of its continuing influence, but also because of the way its adherents (including Marx himself at times) have been systematically unscientific. They have been aware that many of the predictions which Marx made – creditably from a scientific point of view – have been falsified, but, much less creditably they have held on to the theory. They go on devising often spurious explanations for why the theory remains true, despite the failure of its predictions. Among other things Marx predicted that the working class, the proletariat in his terms, would become progressively poorer (more immiserated) under capitalism; that industrial society would become increasingly made up of just two opposed groups, a small capital-owning plutocracy and a vast number of dependent workers; that industrial societies would before long experience socialist revolutions due to the increasingly unbearable tensions between the capitalists and the proletariat; societies would need to go through industrialization before they the revolution to the classless society could come about; and the whole weight of Marx's analysis was on the ever more mighty means of industrial production. Actually, even in Marx's own day, the condition of the workers, bad as it was, was beginning to improve, not only financially, but also socially because of welfare measures introduced by governments. Against Marx's analysis, capitalism or, perhaps better industrial society, was capable of being reformed and improved. Far from industrial societies moving towards two implacably hostile groups, there was in such societies a growing and highly influential middle class of managers, regulators and members of professions. Then, despite some attempts after the First World War, successful communist revolutions have not occurred in capitalist societies. Where communist revolutions have occurred, it has been either in basically agricultural societies, such as Russia and China or through armed forces from outside (in Eastern Europe post-1945). Nor have the Marxist regimes that have appeared shown any tendency to become classless. They have been illiberal and undemocratic dictatorships, with control in the hands of the ruling elite or nomenklatura, with servitude for the majority outside the elite. Indeed today's oligarchs in the Russian Federation have nearly all stemmed from the upper echelons of the former Soviet Union, from its nomenklatura, and similar carve-ups of the society's resources have been seen in the other former Eastern bloc countries. Nor indeed has industrial production been the main engine of historical development, as opposed to consumer satisfaction with ever neater and more materially beneficent devices. Yet Marxists continue at least in a modified form to hold on to their theory, come what may. They say that they can give explanations as to why predictions have not turned out as planned. And they will say that things are not actually so different in the natural science so admired by Popper, where apparent refutations of theories are routinely explained away or even ignored. On this last point, the Marxist view has some plausibility.

    A striking example of this phenomenon was in the early nineteenth century when it appeared that the planet Uranus, at that time the outermost known planet, was not proceeding according to Newtonian principles. It was deviating from its predicted orbit. Yet, far from abandoning their Newtonian framework, two astronomers (Adams and Leverrier) separately postulated that the reason for the apparent irregularity in Uranus's orbit was that there was another, as yet unobserved factor at play. They went on to hypothesize that this interfering factor was an unknown planet beyond Uranus, which was pulling Uranus's orbit out of what it would otherwise have been, and, further, they predicted where and when this unknown body would be observed. Thus Neptune was discovered, triumphantly from the Newtonian perspective, by applying rather than abandoning Newtonian principles. So, the defenders of Marx would say, there is no reason in principle why a scientific theory cannot be saved from apparent refutation by postulating hitherto unknown or unsuspected factors interfering with the data and the predictions. So, when the Marxists defend their theory in this sort of way, as they do, by invoking factors not originally taken into account, *pace* Popper, they are not being unscientific.

The Uranus–Neptune story and the well-known existence of other similar 'savings' of scientific theories have been taken by some to cast doubt on Popper's view of science as working through refutations. It is just not the case that an apparent failure of a theory on some observational prediction either does or should lead to its abandonment. In fact, Popper's own view was never quite as simple as that. From *The Logic of Scientific Discovery* on,[8] he was aware that an apparent refutation of a theory could always be avoided, and sometimes rightly avoided, by invoking a saving hypothesis, as in the Uranus–Neptune case. So the scientific credentials of a theory are not to be seen in consisting purely in producing potential tests. As well as predicting what will count as a test for their theories, scientists have to treat those tests seriously. As happened in the Uranus case, the saving hypothesis itself must produce a testable outcome. In Popper's own terms, the content of a saving hypothesis must be content-increasing, involving new predictions and new tests. Scientific refutability is not merely a matter of what statements follow from a theory; it is a matter of how scientists will treat those statements, and how they will react when a potential refutation has come up. What Popper is insisting here is that scientific practice should be a fundamentally critical practice. When saving hypotheses are rightly invoked to counter what would otherwise be a refutation of a theory, this should be done in a critical spirit, with the saving hypothesis itself being subjected to criticism in terms of its own empirical prediction, as we saw in the case of Uranus and Neptune. The complaint about the Marxists would be that they make life too easy for themselves by not treating their 'explanations' of the failure of the original predictions in a critical spirit. They are seeking simply to save their theories against falsifying evidence, without submitting the saving hypotheses themselves to rigorous testing and taking those further tests seriously.

Popper's view of science then is that it works through proposing testable theories, which is where the Freudians fall down. Where the Marxists (and many others) fall down is that they engage in what Popper calls conventionalism,

---

[8] See Popper (1959), 81–2.

that is, explaining difficulties away without any real increase in predictive content. But, as we have seen, Popper is a resolute critic of inductive inference. So why, even if we have a theory which has survived severe tests in the past, are we entitled to stick with it for the future, and even to rely on it in our actions? Surely this is a form of inductive reasoning: even if we do not consider the theory we are going with verified or confirmed, we are still using our past experience with it to guide our future actions. Is that not what induction is?

Popper's answer to this question strikes many as somewhat evasive, including the present author in his 1980 study of Popper.[9] Popper says that a theory which has survived severe testing can be regarded as what he calls 'well corroborated', and if we are seeking to act or pursue research, there is nothing better to base our activity on than an unrefuted, well-corroborated theory. Here I fear that we move into a somewhat bewildering maze, but there is a simple way out. Both Popper and his critic will agree that the best policy regarding action (and indeed scientific thinking more generally) is to base it on unrefuted, well-corroborated theories; that is, theories which have survived severe testing, do not admit of exceptions, and so on. Popper insists that corroboration is not a species of inductive confirmation or verification. (We should mention here that Popper takes his scepticism about induction to include attempts to declare a successful past theory as probable, as probably a good guide to the future; but even to say that it will probably work in the future is to assume that the future will probably be like the past, or mostly like the past, which is just the point at issue. Was it probable that there were no black swans? And even if our probability logic told us that black swans were highly improbable, that would have availed us little in the event. How can we assume that the future will not be completely different from what we have previously experienced in this or some other matter?)

Well, let us concede to Popper in his refusal to call his method of basing our practice on well-corroborated theories a form of induction. He can call anything what he likes. In typically cavalier style in one of his many discussions of induction and the rationality of apparently inductive reasoning, he says he does 'not regard a fight over the word "rational" as worth spending much time on'.[10] Would he say the same about a quibble over the word 'induction'? From my point of view, what is important in practice is not a quibble over 'induction', but rather that both he and his critic will favour the same theories (unrefuted, severely tested ones). It is beginning to look like a distinction without a difference, both sides making the same recommendations when it comes to the acceptance of a theory. Even so, the critic will continue to insist that there is

---

[9] O'Hear (1980).   [10] Popper (1978), 366.

what Popper once called a 'whiff of verificationism' (or taking the favoured theory to be true on the basis of past experience) in all this, including in Popper's own position. The phrase is to be found in Popper's discussion of his requirement that in the matter of crucial tests the truth content of the new theory must be higher than that of the competitor.[11]

But let us leave the question of Popperian inductivism there, because there is something of great importance underlying his inductive scepticism, something which we should take seriously, beyond any quibbling about words. We should certainly take his 1919 Eddington lesson as seriously as he did. Even the best scientific theory – arguably in this case the best-supported theory of all time – may turn out to be false. And probably will.

Hence Popper's repeated mantra in this area: we can only guess. He did argue that we can know that some guesses are better than others, which seems reasonable, though not always easy to demonstrate in practice. So while we can say that Copernicus's heliocentric theory is better than Ptolemy's geocentrism, Copernicus was actually wrong (the Sun is not the centre of the universe), and there may be aspects of the Ptolemaic system which are worthy of further study, but which have been neglected with the demise of his theory. To take another example, in the study of logic it is generally agreed that the system originating with Russell and Frege is superior to the Aristotelian logic it displaced. Nevertheless, it is arguable that Aristotle does better on nuances of predication, an area where the modern propositional calculus over-simplifies even after a century of more of study[12]. So superseded theories may contain truths and valid perspectives missed in their displacers.

Popper will insist that in the history of modern science, the norm is for a successful and newly accepted theory to contain more truth that its defeated competitor, have more truth-likeness and verisimilitude, as he calls it. Thus Einstein corrects and expands the Newtonian perspective, but contains within itself and in its terms all the truths revealed in Newton. Even if this is something of an idealization, and the new theory only contains most of the truths of the old, it will also typically open us up to new discoveries, unsuspected in the old competitor's account of the universe, which is typically the case, and crucial for the growth of knowledge, which is what we are looking for. Looking back over the history of physics over the past few hundred years, this all seems reasonable. Quantum theory and relativity are huge advances on Newtonian theory and the atomism of the nineteenth century, and have led to spectacular discoveries and innovations and correct predictions of amazing precision. And the same can be

---

[11] Popper (1963), 248 note 31.   [12] See Charlton, (2019).

said of Darwinism and genetic theory, in contrast to pre-evolutionary biology. Admittedly Popper and his followers have had difficulty in working out precisely how verisimilitude is to be defined and how the truth content of a theory is to be analysed and compared to that of another, but let us just say for now that these are largely difficulties of a technical sort. They do not affect the basic point, which is that scientific knowledge has increased exponentially in recent times, with earlier theories being replaced in critical confrontation with their successors as being significantly better both in terms of explanatory power and number and range of successful predictions, as we saw with Einstein and Newton.

However, even if we accept the common-sensical conclusion of the last paragraph, as I think we should, there are still questions to be asked, especially from a Popperian perspective. The first is that a successor theory, Einstein's, say, or Crick and Watson's molecular biology will still itself be subject to problems, obvious and less obvious. Thus we must expect it too eventually to fall like its defeated predecessor (the pessimistic meta-induction!). Tellingly Darwin himself, perhaps the greatest or most successful scientific innovator after Newton himself, speculated that in time natural selection will eventually produce people who would look on himself and the men of his time and their ideas as 'mere barbarians'.[13] This worry is particularly poignant in this context, because Popper himself draws analogies between the critical scientific method and natural selection, with dogmatic thinkers who cannot adapt to new problems suffering the same fate as a species hurtling to extinction as a result of unanticipated selective pressure from the environment.[14]

Of course the natural selection analogy is not exact, and in one significant respect would be misleading. For the member of a pre-human biological species confronted by an environmental problem it cannot adapt to will die, as will the species as a whole if there are no helpful mutations along the way. But in science, and human culture more generally, our theories and ideas are not internally programmed by an unalterable genetic structure. Our theories are objective, outside of us. They are written down and can be studied and altered or even rejected, as the environment requires, without our bodily constitution being affected. As Popper liked to put it, the ability to express and write down our theories exosomatically, and so subject them to the critical method, means that, alone in the world we inhabit, we can let our theories die in our stead.

So the critical-scientific method gives humans an immense advantage in the struggle for existence. But, survival advantage apart, the critical method, in Popper's view, does not make even our best-tested theory any more likely to be

---

[13] See Darwin (1903), 30 (letter of C. Darwin to Lyell, 27 April 1860).
[14] See Popper (1992), 44–52.

true. Just as much as any species in the animal kingdom, a theory that is successful for a time is destined for eventual extinction or, more accurately refutation and replacement by a better theory. Hard as it may be to admit it from our position of vast scientific expertise and research and of much apparent success, for Popper we cannot know, we can only guess. Thus, reporting on his decades-old view in 1983, Popper wrote: if 'to "know" means ... to be in possession of *sufficient reason* for holding that our knowledge is true and certain, ... there was no such thing as scientific knowledge ... scientific knowledge was not a species of knowledge ... measured by the high standards of scientific criticism, "scientific knowledge" always remained sheer guess-work – although guesswork controlled by criticism and experiment'.[15] Popper calls his refusal to think of any theory, however successful, as the ultimate and incontrovertible truth anti-essentialism. He believes that we will never uncover the final essence of the way the universe works.

Does Popper exaggerate here? It may be that we don't and can't hope to know very much about the further reaches of string theory or cosmic antimatter. It may be that at various points we brush against the limits of human intelligence and intellectual capacity, as Niels Bohr thought was the case with quantum theory. (The apparently solution-resistant paradoxes of the quantum world may show that Bohr was not being over-modest about our intellectual powers here, despite the phenomenal predictive success of quantum theory. We may just not know what type of reality we are talking about in the quantum world, even if we can predict to a startling degree of accuracy what will happen there). However, we do know an awful lot about the more mundane aspects of the material world, and about the theories governing such things as aero-flight, the human genome and nuclear power. And by 'know', I do mean know and not just guess, which would imply that the next time someone takes off to a sunny clime on a budget airline, he is not merely wagering on the outcome with his life. There is a slight risk, to be sure, but, what rightly gives him confidence here are theories, low-level theories maybe, but theories nonetheless, and theories which have been found satisfactory in innumerable instances of flight over a century or more. Popper's 'only guessing' here seems hyperbolic, if not actually a misuse of language. Again it may be that sometime in the future all this understanding of how flight works may let us down, and so we may refrain from calling it knowledge in an absolute sense. But it is not *mere* guess-work. Popper needs a category of epistemic confidence somewhere between knowledge in the full sense and mere (?) guesswork.

---

[15] Popper (1983), 12–13.

On the other hand, there is something compelling about Popper's scepticism about basic, fundamental theory, about his anti-essentialism, in other words. Our picture of how the world is either at the microscopic level or at the level of cosmology is forever uncertain and revisable, as well as leaving the current fundamental principles themselves unexplained. The history of the mature sciences does not look like a steady progression along a smooth trajectory. And the underlying conceptions of just how the world is in whatever area of existence do seem to undergo dramatic revolutions in what has been called the paradigm, or general set of assumptions about entities and powers and indeed about the nature and structure of the world itself, maybe as radical in their way as the differences among the pre-Socratics. Popper will explain these revolutions in approaches to the subject matter in terms of his critical approach: theories which fail severe tests being replaced by often radically different conceptions, which lead to new discoveries *and* problems. The reason for the new problems is that no theory ever meshes seamlessly with the world it is describing and explaining. In developing the new paradigm all sorts of unexpected insights and questions arise, including new problems for the scientists involved to tackle. In investigating these new problems new refutations will almost certainly bubble up, if the scientists are being sufficiently critical, and so the whole cycle will begin all over again.

There is indeed something compelling about this Popperian approach to the history of science, even in the somewhat simplified version of the last paragraph. But is it correct? Here we touch on the famous, or infamous, confrontation between Popper and his former student Thomas Kuhn back in 1965. Kuhn, it will be recalled, published his phenomenally influential *The Structure of Scientific Revolutions* in 1962, which had seemed to many to undermine the whole Popperian picture.[16] Normally, Kuhn argued, scientists are not trying to falsify or refute the theories with which they are working. They work within what he called a paradigm, a set of basic assumptions and theories which specify the nature of the entities they are looking at, what sorts of things they were, and how we should go about looking into them. Normally, in a mature science, people simply accept the paradigm within which they had been trained. They know that there were always difficulties and failures thrown up by the paradigm, but these are not treated as falsifications or refutations. They are regarded as 'problems' to be solved, within the paradigm – with luck and ingenuity in the way it happened with Uranus and Neptune. But, continuing that story, when Mercury's orbit was also seen as deviant, another planet, between the Sun and Mercury, was postulated, actually by Leverrier, one of Neptune's discoverers. It was named Vulcan. But,

---

[16] Kuhn (1962).

unlike Neptune, Vulcan was not discovered, for the simple reason it did not exist. Nevertheless despite this fact, well known in the nineteenth century, until Einstein arrived in the twentieth with what Kuhn would call a different paradigm, the failure to observe Vulcan did not shake the confidence of the scientific community in Newton. It was only when a revolutionary paradigm – Einstein's – came along that the move was made in the Einsteinian direction. And not all scientists accepted this; for a decade or more some prominent researchers continued to defend Newton, until, as Kuhn put it, that generation died out.

In Kuhn's picture, there are at least two elements which seem to be in tension with Popper's view. One is that Kuhn appears to argue that the transition between one paradigm and another cannot be seen as a fully rational process. This is because defenders of the old paradigm can always continue to defend their paradigm and hope that eventually enough saving hypotheses will emerge. The Newtonian die-hards were not irrational but were acting genuinely scientifically. So paradigm change seems to have elements of fashion and group behaviour about it, when the young Turks of the new paradigm eventually win the battle of taste against the old guard. More fundamentally Kuhn thinks of two competing paradigms in a case such as this as being mutually incommensurable: their presuppositions and methods of investigation are so different as to preclude unbiased comparison.

Popper will respond to this latter point by saying that Kuhn and his followers (or whom there are many, especially in the soft social sciences) are imprisoned in what he calls the myth of the framework. Each party is so rooted in competing and conflicting worldviews that impartial comparison cannot be made, because each will see the world in their own terms, and translate what the opponent puts forward into those terms. What is presented as counter-evidence is thus turned into support for their own position. Popper argued against this that while there are occasions where two competing theories or world views might seem at first sight to be incommensurable, we are never wholly imprisoned within our own framework or world view. As he puts it, culture clash can actually be fruitful, where each party to a dispute stands outside their own presuppositional cage and looks from a new perspective. From this higher viewpoint, both can begin to establish common ground between the two initially radically opposed positions. Indeed Popper is emphatic that the more difference there is in the background of arguers, and presumably the greater distance there is between their positions, the more fruitful the argument. Not even a common language is necessary. Diversity and attempts to build mutual comprehension are what makes critical argument enlightening.

As far as the history of science goes, it is hard to accept the Kuhnian view that there is ever complete breakdown of communication between holders of different paradigms. At a lower, observational level there is always a sense that each paradigm is attempting to account for the same phenomena, even if the terms in which they are being described and understood are different. Without the sense that we were all trying to explain the same things, we would have to ask a disagreement about what. No doubt Ptolemy had a completely different understanding of what a planet is from Newton or from today's astronomers. Yet when he talked about Mars and its sphere, he was still talking about the same red planet and its orbit, and indeed we will say that he was wrong about *it*, the same it, where we have better knowledge. Otherwise we could hardly begin to understand the Ptolemaic system, or even to see what it was supposedly explaining, and how it disagrees with our picture of the solar system and is less reliable than it. The fact that we can all agree that we are talking about the same thing when Mars is mentioned is what ties us all down to a common foundation.

So there are significant differences between Popper and Kuhn (and places where we will say the balance lies with Popper). But more surprising, and more important, is the extent to which they actually agree. As we have just seen, Kuhn thinks when scientists work unquestioningly within the paradigm is the norm, hence he calls it 'normal' science. Nor should we despise normal science. Working within a paradigm leads to all sorts of discoveries and innovations, as the paradigm yields the secrets its way of thinking points to. But, according to Kuhn, when a paradigm begins to run out of steam, difficulties and problems outweighing successes, the scientific community is ready for a new paradigm, which seems to solve the old problems in a new way and to promise expansion of knowledge elsewhere. This will be the period of what Kuhn calls extraordinary or revolutionary science, a period of excitement, upheaval and controversy, which dominates until the new paradigm settles down into its normal phase.

Kuhn's revolutionary science is strikingly like the Popperian model of no holds-barred severe testing and refutation producing major theoretical advances. But it is not the case that Popper denies that there is such a thing as Kuhnian normal science, or indeed that normal science is not for a lot of the time the norm. So, 'normally', for both Popper and Kuhn, scientists do not act in an extraordinary revolutionary way, testing their paradigmatic framework to destruction. They work within it, bound by 'a structure of scientific doctrines already in existence'. The words are not Kuhn's, but Popper's, from his 1934 preface to the original edition of *The Logic of Scientific Discovery*.[17] There is

---

[17] Popper (1959), xxx.

also this account of revolutionary science as 'a method which destroys, changes, and alters, the whole thing, including its most important instrument, the language in which our myths and theories are formulated'. The words look just like Kuhn, in writing about paradigm change. But they are actually Popper's from 1948, sometime before Kuhn had started writing.[18]

The difference between Popper and Kuhn on the fundamental matter of normal and extraordinary science is not even that one is normal and the other extraordinary. Normal science certainly exists, for both Popper and Kuhn. The difference between them is whether the normality of normal science is a good thing or not. *Pace* Kuhn, and perhaps *pace* his own 1934 preface, by the time Popper had come to debate with Kuhn in 1965: 'I can only say that I see a very great danger in it . . . just as I see a great danger in the increase of specialization, which also is an undeniable historical fact: a danger to science and, indeed, to our civilization'.[19] A danger to our civilization, maybe hyperbolic, but deeply felt by Popper, because it is a complete repudiation of the critically infused science which he sees as the most important feature of Western civilization since the Enlightenment. What should be the leading edge and exemplar of the critical approach he so values itself succumbs to a mind-numbing dogmatism and institutional conformity. And who, looking at the institution of science as it is today, with its funding and promotion models, its peer-review and paradigm-enforcing pedagogy, its systems of honours and the shutting out of dissentient voices, is to say that Popper is completely wrong? Of course, one could say that all this is actually a good thing, or the only way science nowadays can exist and develop, but what one certainly cannot say is that this is the science Popper valued so highly.

I will end this brief account of Popperian philosophy of science by saying something about his view 'experts' and of claims to expertise, because this will lead us nicely into our analysis of his social and political philosophy. We have already seen that Popper is opposed to specialization, presumably the sort of specialization which makes it impossible for the specialist to communicate with anyone outside the specialization. In like manner he also waged a lifelong war against technical language, except where it was essential, and, needless to say, against professionally exclusive jargon as well. But over and above these somewhat mundane requirements for clarity and openness, he also inveighs against experts. He 'disbelieves in specialization and experts. By paying too much respect to the specialist, we are destroying the commonwealth of learning, the rationalist tradition, and science itself'.[20] Too often claims to expertise will be techniques to exclude disagreement and criticism of a radical sort, just what

---

[18] Popper (1963), 129.   [19] Lakatos and Musgrave (1971), 53.   [20] Popper (1983), 8.

would be needed to advance scientific knowledge in Popper's full-blooded revolutionary sense.

But, as we show in the next section, Popper requires full-blooded criticism in political matters as well, even if, for reasons of humanity he eschews revolution in the social sphere. There are nevertheless close similarities between his views on science and those on society. In both spheres, he inveighs against the dogmatism and complacency of 'experts'. In neither does he think we will even find certainty. In both he sees an element of human striving to go beyond where we are, and he introduces elements of humility and humanitarianism to colour our admirable striving to improve. In the scientific case this is to delve deeper into the mysteries of the universe, but he warns us that to be clear 'about our present limitations' in this respect, 'certain things at least now look as if they are eternal mysteries'.[21] In the political sphere, our aim should be to produce a more humane life for free individuals throughout society. In both enterprises there are elements derived from his 1919 experiences, which also sit well with his own brand of religiousness, with his conception of what human beings are and should be.

3 Social and Political Philosophy

If Popper's reputation among professional philosophers rests firmly on his philosophy of science, among the general educated public he is probably better known as a political thinker, renowned among other things for his devastating attack on the influence of Karl Marx, and on the pretensions of his followers to know the way history is going. As I have already intimated, there is not such a big disjunction between his ideas on science and those on politics. Both can be seen as applications of his critical rationalism, of the idea that human progress, whether in scientific knowledge or in social and political affairs, is secured by means of the testing of ideas and the replacement of one failing approach by one that promises to solve the problems of its predecessor. Indeed the parallel between science and politics in Popper's thought is close enough to suggest that the ideal political society is in many ways like the ideal scientific community. In both cases, the 'normal' or the same as what has gone before is markedly inferior to a situation in which criticism is welcomed and listened to, and, as appropriate, acted upon. I shall have more to say on this point later, and in particular, the way in which Popper does see the need for tradition in a healthy political regime. I will also stress the way in which Popper sees Western democratic society as an unprecedented success in the history of the world, just as he sees the science which arose from the Western scientific revolution of

---

[21] Popper (1957), iii.

the seventeenth century as unprecedented and unique, though also now available and to a large extent followed throughout the rest of the world.

Although as we have seen already the seed of Popper's approach to social and political affairs was sown as early as 1919, following his experience with revolutionary communists, he actually developed his political thought mainly during the Second World War, while he was living and working in New Zealand. This resulted in two books, *The Open Society and Its Enemies* and *The Poverty of Historicism*. The latter, though not published as a book until 1957, had been started in the mid 1930s and it actually appeared as a journal article in 1944 and 1945, which was the same year as *The Open Society* was published. Together they formed what Popper was later to call his 'war work'. But they were far more than that.

To see why Popper's political writings were so important at the time, we must remember that during the Second World War Britain and the United States were allied with Soviet Russia. Despite the horrors of the Soviet regime in the 1920s and 1930s, there was considerable admiration for communist Russia in the West during the war, particularly among intellectuals, propagandists in the army education units and journalists. The gulags, the Ukrainian famine and the show trials were overlooked by many, no doubt because few took note of them in the first place. There were also plenty of Moscow-based journalists and intellectuals at home only too ready to extol the tawdry virtues of Lenin and the Soviet system. In the mid-1940s there were just a handful of writers who warned against this and indeed against communism in general. Of these the four most notable were George Orwell (*Animal Farm*), Hayek (*The Road to Serfdom*), Arthur Koestler (*Darkness at Noon*), and Popper himself. Orwell had encountered the duplicity of communism at first hand in the Spanish Civil War, as is well known, but he had difficulty in getting *Animal Farm* published in Britain in 1945. Koestler, a former communist, was an émigré Hungarian, and later an intellectual gadfly. Hayek and Popper were Viennese, with personal experience of both fascism and communism. All four were thus more knowledgeable about European totalitarianism than most people in Britain and the US at the time. And, as we have seen, Hayek was crucial to getting Popper's *Open Society* published, also to getting Popper to come to London in 1946, after which they remained close friends and allies in the struggle against the still dominant doctrinaire leftism of the post-war academic world.

3.1 Historicism

There were two fundamental planks to Popper's political thinking. The first was impassioned advocacy of what he called the open society. The second was an equally impassioned hostility to what he called historicism, by which he meant the belief that history had a definite direction, and one which we (or the enlightened among us) could discern. His almost visceral dislike of historicism comes out forcefully in his dedication to *The Poverty of Historicism*: 'In memory of the countless men and women of all creeds or nations or races who fell victim to the fascist and communist belief in Inexorable Laws of Historical Destiny'.[22]

To show how seriously Popper took his anti-historicism, as we may call it, it is fascinating to note that he saw even the history of art as being distorted in recent times by the way artists have been persuaded that they have a mission to keep up with the times, even to be ahead of their time: 'Whoever has seen the great works of the past – Michelangelo's, for instance – must admit that there has been a decline in art. Obviously Michelangelo was and will remain the greatest and we cannot expect anything like that to-day. But what is the reason for the general decline in art? It is because all artists hear what historicists predict about the future, and then, instead of trying to create good work, they concentrate on being leaders for the future ... they listen to bad prophets, bad philosophers, who themselves try to be ahead of their time'.[23] If anyone wants to question what Popper is saying here about the historicist tendency of the contemporary art world, they should simply go into a gallery of contemporary art and look not just at the works being displayed, which will show scant regard to the achievements of the past – Michelangelo might not have lived – but also at the accompanying mind destroying commentaries by critics and curators.

What Popper says about Michelangelo he would also have said about Bach, whom he revered, and about music post Schoenberg, whose advanced 'Private Performances' of the new atonal music Popper attended without being convinced. No doubt we could say the same about modernistic architecture, which had its origins in Vienna and other parts of the Austro-Hungarian Empire. (Indeed I did, in my paper entitled 'Historicism and Architectural Knowledge'[24]). In all these areas, as Popper says, everyone is striving to be up to date, to break with the past, and will dismiss any of their contemporaries who are so blind to the necessities of history that they continue to build in classical or gothic style, or to compose tonal music. (See e.g. the scorn with which Pierre Boulez dismissed contemporary music which was not according to the dogmas of his school.)

But as Popper, who was in Vienna when many of these trends got a foothold, points out, in reality, no one is in a position to anticipate the future. The most fundamental reason for this is that what we think about any matter itself affects our behaviour. This in turn will itself affect the future, and in ways we can never fully accommodate in our thinking. One example of this phenomenon is the

---

[22] Popper (1997), 41.   [23] Popper and Eccles (1977), 20.   [24] O'Hear, 1993.

Oedipus effect, which Popper discusses in an article designed to show that even a classical Newtonian physics cannot be wholly deterministic.[25] Oedipus was told by the oracle that he was going to kill his father and marry his mother. So he took steps to falsify the oracle's prediction, which led directly to his killing his father and marrying his mother (who were not the people he believed them to be). Had he known that, he might have taken steps to avoid going to Thebes, where his real father and mother actually were. He could then have returned to Corinth where the people he wrongly believed to be his parents were; but again that would have set up a new situation, whose outcome would not be encompassed in the prediction about the need to avoid going to Thebes, and so on and so on, recursively. In every attempt to falsify a prediction, there will be outcomes that are not yet predicted; in our stream of predictions about the results of earlier predictions, we will never be able to catch up with the results of the latest predictions in our series. This is putting the matter in an individualistic way, but the same point will apply to large-scale predictions of the future. Attempting to predict the way these predictions will themselves influence the future will once again be an unending and unfulfillable process, which no planner can fully accommodate in his plans.

This somewhat abstract line of thought is given a highly pertinent concrete application in the Preface to *The Poverty of Historicism*.[26] There Popper points out that the development of human history is strongly influenced by the growth of human knowledge, including the growth of our scientific and technological ideas. However, it is impossible now to predict just what this growth will be in the future or what it will lead to. If we could accurately predict these future innovations now, we would know them and develop them now. They would not be future developments, about which we would still be in the dark. To illustrate this point, consider Alan Turing's development of the code-breaking computer back in the 1940s. Could anyone then have predicted the smart phone of today, let alone its multifarious applications, many of whose consequences we hardly understand even today? Even less could anyone, even Turing himself, have foreseen that his successful code-breaking apparatus, the gigantic and unwieldy Bletchley 'Colossus', could have been an application of his earlier highly abstract and apparently purely theoretical research into mathematical provability (on Hilbert's so-called *Entscheidungsproblem*) in the late 1930s.

Popper's point is that if there is such a thing as growth in human knowledge, which there surely is, then we cannot anticipate today what we shall know only tomorrow. A human scientist or calculating machine, he goes on to say, cannot possibly predict, by scientific methods, its own future results. This lack of

---

[25] Popper (1950). [26] Popper (1957), v–vii.

predictability does not apply only to scientific and technological developments. An example of a more general unpredictability dear to Popper's own heart would be the emergence of Winston Churchill as Prime Minister in 1940. He saved Western civilization, according to Popper, having been the only man who understood what was happening in the 1930s.[27] During this time, in which he was in the political wilderness, he was actually writing a huge biography of his ancestor John Churchill, the first Duke of Marlborough, the doing of which made him all the more sensitive to the danger of a pan-European despotism. In the earlier case, the potential despot was not Hitler, but Louis XIV, whom the earlier Churchill saw off in the so-called War of Spanish Succession, starting with his inspired victory at Blenheim which completely wrong-footed the French who were mainly stuck in Flanders. But John Churchill aside, it is frightening to think what might have happened if Winston Churchill, this extraordinary and unpredictable maverick, clearly a man from an earlier epoch, unabashedly out of tune with the history of his day let alone its future direction, not been able to take over the reins of power in Britain during the Second World War.

Even admitting that there are intractable difficulties for the agent who attempts to predict their own future or that of their society, it might still be said that there are trends in history, which are evident in its general direction. Much of the case of the historicist rests on a claim to discern trends in the past which will continue in the future. The Marxist picture is precisely a picture of that sort, which enables its adherents to condemn, theoretically or physically, those not marching in line with what they see as history's direction. Ideas of this sort are extremely common, extending into art history as we have seen. Nor are they confined to leftists, as anyone who remembers Francis Fukuyama's Hegelian claim back in 1992 that the fall of the Berlin Wall presaged the end of history will appreciate.[28] Inspired by Hegelian thinking Fukuyama claimed that history in a sense would end with the spread of parliamentary democracy throughout the world: no more tribal, monarchical, aristocratic or dictatorial governments, but a mild, prosperous and peace-loving world in which all countries would pursue prosperity rather than war, with benign, welfarist conditions at home. Ironic, perhaps, that Fukuyama's well-meaning and up to a point well-argued vision was put forward just before countries from China to Russia to various Islamic and African countries decided that history definitely would go on for some time yet in rather different directions: appalling turmoil in the Middle East, Islamic fundamentalists again dominant in Afghanistan, a Russia bent on recovering its pride and territory, and a non-democratic

---

[27] Popper (1992), 112.   [28] Fukuyama (1992).

China looking to become the major economic power in the world if America cannot halt it. History has very much not ended.

Fukuyama had discerned a trend towards liberal democracy, but it was a trend which was derailed by what a hitherto successful British prime minister, dislodged by scandals among his ministers, is reputed to have described as 'events, dear boy, events'. In other words, specific and unplanned for circumstances upsetting the best-laid plans of peoples and their rulers, in this case, his. One of his ministers, during his tenure of office, claimed not unreasonably the population as a whole had 'never had it so good', but that counted for nothing when the scandals in question dominated political discourse.

That, in crude essence, is Popper's point. We can indeed see trends in the past, retrospectively, as we cast our eyes over what has happened and the reasons why we are where we are now. But in doing this, we forget that what happened in the past was crucially affected by specific and unique circumstances. There are general laws governing social and economic affairs, but these will be general and comparatively bland. Popper gives as examples laws such as 'you cannot introduce agricultural tariffs and at the same time reduce the cost of living', or 'you cannot have a centrally planned society with a price system that fulfils the main functions of competitive prices', or 'you cannot have full employment without inflation', or 'you cannot make a revolution without causing a reaction'. These and similar laws, if true are important, and are often ignored. But they are entirely general, whereas what are crucial in the course of human affairs are the particular circumstances obtaining at any moment, and these are by definition unique and unrepeatable. The theorist of trends fails to see how the pattern he sees in the past is far more influenced by particular events and circumstances, which he tends to discount, than by any general laws which apply to the circumstances. Arguably this points to a difference between scientific and historical explanations. With scientific explanations, particularly in laboratory conditions, particular circumstances can often be overlooked as unimportant, because they do not vary much in different times and places. With historical explanations, by contrast, the particular circumstances and context of an event are all important. The historicist in seeing a general direction to history, and claiming knowledge for it, is confusing context-dependent trends for laws.

As well as confusing trends and laws the historicist is, in Popper's view, in an objectionable sense a holist. By this he means that the historicist, like the 1919 Viennese communists, focuses on society as a whole, rather than seeing as composed of individual men and women, whose particular lives and sufferings and aspirations should be taken into account, and regarded as having worth and validity. In his holism the historicist, such as Popper's contemporary Karl Mannheim, will typically tend to identify society with the state, like the

Marxists advocating extending the power of the state until the identity becomes well-nigh complete.[29] Popper does not deny that a society is a system, but he is fiercely resistant to the holistic notion that the system should be seen as more important than and superior to the individuals who compose the system, or indeed that autonomous institutions in a society should be taken over by the state, as they were in Soviet Russia. The holist, of whom, as we will shortly see Plato and Marx might be taken as prime examples, sees the individual as defined by his or her position and status in society, and is required to fulfil that role or function irrespective of his or her feelings, beliefs or desires.

A consequence of the holistic approach to society and politics is the conviction that a society can and should be organized and redesigned as a whole through top-down engineering in which the component parts (in this case individual people) are treated as no more than cogs or screws in a greater whole, which is the state. This might recall to mind Ruskin's famous accusation that in the division of labour he so deprecated men were 'divided into mere segments of men – broken into small fragments and crumbs of life ... (so that all) that is left in a man is not enough to make a pin or a nail, but exhausts itself into making the point of a pin or the head of a nail'.[30]

Popper's holist is not the Bradford factory owner Ruskin was attacking or the Bounderby of Dickens' *Hard Times*. He was or is a Utopian, an ostensibly well-meaning reformer or revolutionary who wants to make all things new and better (though it is worth remembering that some of the factory owners Ruskin was attacking were actually well-meaning folk, ostensibly devout Christians and Quakers, who thought that their factories and the towns they built around them were improving the conditions of their pin-point and nail-head makers). The Popperian utopian's ambitions and methods are, from Popper's point of view, objectionable on two significant fronts.

The first is that utopians are so enamoured of their holistic blueprints that they fail to recognize that all human planning and effort has unintended consequences, many of which will be unforeseen and some unwanted. Utopians fail, in other words, at the first stage of the critical approach. Convinced, as Plato and Marx and their followers were, of the intellectual correctness of their plan, instead of abandoning the utopian blueprint in the face of difficulties, they will double down on it, whereas, as we will see in the next section Popper advocates what he calls piecemeal social engineering. This is an approach to social and political problems which takes them one by one, and carefully and critically evaluating the effects of these reform. Perhaps even worse than their holistic approach to society and its reform, utopians will typically accuse critics

---

[29] See Popper (1957), 67. [30] Ruskin (1985), 87.

of intellectual and moral turpitude, as we saw in Soviet Russia. And this brings us on to the second way in which utopians are likely to be objectionable from Popper's point of view. They will dismiss any who criticize as being out of tune with the times, and insensitive to the way history is going. Both of these reactions manifest a dismissal of the individual subject of the utopian society, and all too often a not purely theoretical dismissal. They also manifest on the part of the utopian planners and politicians imperviousness to criticism as they throw at their opponents the accusation of being out of step with the age. Such attitudes are characteristic of the enemies of Popper's open society, to which we now turn.

3.2 The Open Society

Popper's *magnum opus* on social and political philosophy is called *The Open Society and Its Enemies*. It would not be unfair to say that the two volumes of this work are far more about the enemies of the open society than about the open society itself, and specifically about two enemies, Plato and Marx (though Aristotle and Hegel do get passing somewhat inadequate treatment). Why Plato and Marx, one might wonder; surely fascism in the early 1940s merited a demolition as much as Marx. Maybe Popper thought that Aurel Kolnai, a neglected Hungarian émigré, had said all that needed to be said on that score in his 1938 *tour de force The War Against the West*, which Popper much admired.[31] Or maybe he thought that with the erosion and impending defeat of Nazism, the main danger to the open society was Marxist communism, about to take over half of Europe and many other places too. Also, Plato and Marx were clearly more formidable enemies intellectually speaking than the rag-taggle pronouncements of Mussolini, Hitler and their antecedents and followers.

Plato and Marx supplied formidable cases for the need for any good society to be under the rule of intellectuals, who alone understood deep truths about human nature and society, and for the need for them, the intellectuals, to organize society holistically for the good of each and all. I will not say much here about Popper's direct critique of Plato and Marx. I have already written briefly about why Popper thinks that Marx and Marxist are not scientific, while much of his discussion of Plato spells out the totalitarian aspects of Plato's political writings, particularly in *Republic,* distinguishing Plato's views from those of Socrates (which Popper much admired as early examples of the critical attitude). This campaign of Popper's has been bitterly contested by a number of Platonists. But it is hard for the dispassionate observer to be convinced that

---

[31] Kolnai (1938).

Popper has got Plato completely or even partly wrong, however much one wants to excuse Plato for his uncritical adulation of a polity modelled on the lines of a purified Sparta or Crete and his corresponding distaste for Periclean and democratic Athens after what Athens did to Socrates. Plato's brilliant insights into the mentality flourishing in different types of polity, rule by one, rule by a few and rule by the many, in a way simply make his positive prescriptions for a good society the more tempting and the more dangerous.

However intellectual utopians are not the only enemies of the open society. There is also tribal society, which Popper sees as characterized by a rigid and unthinking adherence to tribal myths and practices, and a tendency to exclude and persecute any who are unfaithful to the tribe: 'Social life is determined by social and religious taboos; everybody has his assigned place within the whole of the social structure; everyone feels that his place is the "natural" place, assigned to him by the forces which rule the world; everyone "knows his place"'.[32] In that sense, of course, the majority of humankind has always lived in a tribal society, and, Fukuyama notwithstanding, many still do. If one wants a short account of the open society desired by Popper, a good start would be the negation of everything in the sentence just quoted, adding to that Popper's earlier insistence that in a tribal society the individual, along with his or her reason and dignity, counts for is nothing. The tribe is supremely important. And even in societies which are no longer literally tribalist there may still be an element of collectivism, in which the individual is defined not by his or her identity but by the group or collective with which he or she is identified.[33] These aspects of tribalism are often combined with a historicist and utopian belief in the chosenness of that group, whether religious, racial, economic or classist, and now sexual, or a combination of several of these characteristics. This way of thinking, now called identitarianism and usually connected to some sense of victimhood, has made an unwelcome re-appearance in recent times. That this is happening some seven or eight decades after Popper wrote about tribalism and its denial of the worth of the individual should surely give us pause.

It is, though, surprising that in discussing the enemies of the open society, Popper says virtually nothing about tribalism, beyond making the very general points in the last paragraph. Yet when writing *The Open Society* he was actually living in the midst of a tribal society. For he was on South Island, New Zealand, and in the land of the Maori Ngai Tahu tribe. Various reasons of a largely personal nature have been adduced for this perplexing silence on Popper's part but rather than speculating on these, there is a more important point to be made.

---

[32] Popper (1966), vol. I, 12.   [33] See Popper (1966), vol. I, 316.

In 2002 at the Popper centenary celebrations in Vienna, I met Te Maire Tau, a leading member of the Ngai Tahu tribe. He was there as a student and admirer of Popper's work and philosophy. I then went on to a similar event being held in Christchurch NZ for the same reason, and when there Professor Te Maire Tau, as he now is, was kind enough to introduce me to other members of the tribe and to invite me to attend a marae (a restricted tribal meeting) in Christchurch.

Why this anecdote is significant here is because Te Maire's view, along with other leading Ngai Tahu, was that, following Popper's lead, the tribe should seek to move into the open society. Indeed they were already doing that with some success, having made their peace with the New Zealand government at the long-running Waitangi Tribunal which was supposed to redress the wrongs done to the Maoris in the 1840s, when they were effectively cheated and robbed by the so-called Waitangi Treaty. Having settled, the Ngai Tahu had then set up prosperous businesses in Christchurch and other places on the South Island. However at the time, and to an extent still today, among some Maoris there was a view that they and their children should enclose themselves in rigid tribal customs and lore. Not only is this the opposite of openness, but in the view of my Ngai Tahu friends this is the best possible way to keep Maori society in a deprived and welfare-dependent state. The Ngai Tahu wanted their children to be educated in such a way as to enter the larger open society as seamlessly as possible, to engage with it and its benefits, and certainly not to be enclosed in an inward-facing tribal mentality.

But this need not mean that one abandons one's tribal heritage either for oneself or for one's children, who should still be taught about it, while also getting the same lessons as the rest of the population in the rest of the curriculum, with a solid cultural grounding and in subjects such as science, engineering and law. Thus, for example, given that New Zealand is a constitutional monarchy based on the Westminster system, it is important that everyone there is given a basic understanding of the English history in which that system developed. But equally, everyone in New Zealand could or should be given some insight into the meaning of custom, or tikanga, as it developed in the Maori tradition.

The marae that I attended was fascinating for at least two reasons. One was that at it we were studying Polynesian myths and the way that these had been brought to New Zealand a thousand years or so ago when groups of humans reached the islands from their homes thousands of miles away in the South Pacific (itself an achievement of some magnitude given the canoes in which they travelled and the extent of their knowledge as to where they were going). These Polynesian myths had over the years been adapted so as to reflect the topography of South Island, while still keeping to their basic characters and themes. The second point was that the Ngai Tahu myths and customs had themselves evolved somewhat further over the 150 years or so that the white settlers had observed them and written them down. In other words, tribal customs and myths, far from being set in stone and reflecting some primeval past, as some might think, are subject to continual evolutionary modification in the light of circumstances, a process made the more fluid in the absence of written records. Without such records, no one knows exactly what the original New Zealand settlers from Polynesia thought and believed hundreds of years ago even though we have some idea of the basic stories (some of which are still current in the far-off Polynesian islands, which is what became clear in the marae I attended).

But the other general point to be made here is that what I saw in Christchurch showed that it was possible to study and respect one's tribal roots without cutting oneself off from openness and the open society. This, of course, required a spirit of magnanimity and reconciliation on the part of the Ngai Tahu, because there is no doubt that the Maoris in general had been cheated when they supposedly placed themselves under the British crown in the Treaty of Waitangi in 1840. But the question in the twenty-first century is how best to deal with the situation as it exists now, and the Ngai Tahu had decided the best thing was to make the best of both worlds, their own and the wider society. In other words, *pace* Popper, it is possible to be a member of both a tribal and an open society. And, one could add to that the idea that the larger New Zealand society should also recognize in a spirit of openness that it might have things to learn from the older inhabitants of the islands, a point Popper might well have endorsed owing to his hostility to the idea that one is enclosed in a mental framework from which one cannot or should not emerge.

In turning to the non-tribal enemies of the open society, we need first to say something about what Popper means by an open society. The open society he advocates is primarily one in which institutions and policies are subject to critical assessment and evaluation. This is because any policy or institution, however beneficent in intention (and of course not all are), will be subject to unforeseen consequences. Not even the best-informed legislator can know in advance just how his or her policies are going to work out in practice. This is partly because of the obstacles to knowing the future we have already considered, but to them, we can also add and underline the impact of human freedom on any plan that is introduced. We cannot know in advance precisely or even broadly how people, individually or collectively, are going to react to a plan or a policy or even to a new product launched on the market. Popper is a firm believer in human freedom, an indeterminist as we will see further in the next section. Human choices and decisions always have an element of unpredictability about them, which of course compounds the difficulty of knowing what the consequences of any plan or policy affecting individual people.

It is just this uncertainty which the theorist of the closed society will deny. He or she 'knows' the direction of history, in the Marxist case towards a utopian state, or a perfect system in which the state itself withers away as unnecessary. In the less than utopian world we currently inhabit, force will be needed to ensure that no one impedes the march towards utopia. For Plato utopia will be achieved not by the march of history but by a myth (or noble lie) by means of which the different classes of people in society will be kept in strict order according to the class to which they belong by the philosopher rulers with the support of the guardian police. But Plato does not explain how the utopia he wants will be brought about (though he does suggest that once achieved, it will eventually degenerate, which may be heartening from a Popperian perspective). The Marxist prescription is seemingly more realistic. Between the present imperfect state of class division and the future society of perfect freedom, the proletariat will revolt against the capitalist rulers, and set up its own dictatorship. This dictatorship will change society and the human beings living in it along the lines of enforced equality and central control and distribution of resources. Equality having been achieved and planning perfected, eventually there will be no need for any authority or government. The truly classless, peace-loving society will enjoy the fruits of the earth in an equitable fashion without the need of force or compulsion.

Plato bases his ideal society, or the run up to it on a lie. But one of the features of revolutionary Marxist activity Popper noted back in 1919 was that actual policies changed from day to day. The leaders were unashamed in lying about this or about other things supposedly necessary for the cause. This was justifiable because the end (Marxist revolution) was supremely good. What was needed for it trumped every other consideration, which justified not only the sacrifice of life and individual freedom, but also of truth. That Popper noticed and deplored this very early in his life no doubt goes some way to explaining Vaclav Havel's admiration for Popper. It also underpins his own stinging first-hand indictment of communism as a matter of ordinary people being willing in their daily life to live within the lie, the lie, that is, which permeates the whole communist project.[34]

Popper's open society is crucially a matter of living in the truth, to borrow the title of Havel's own book. *Living in Truth*, or what Popper might call living with or in the critical attitude, which means subjecting one's own beliefs to testing,

---

[34] See Havel (1986), 50–51.

considering alternative points of view, engaging with people from other perspectives, and giving up one's beliefs when they are shown to be wrong. Popper himself describes the critical approach thus: we go from a problem to a tentative solution or solutions, we then eliminate error(s) to our solution(s) as far as we can, which takes us to a second problem or set of problems, and the cycle repeats, endlessly. We have already seen at length that in science this means that we subject our theories to severe testing and modify or give them up when this fails.

This schema can easily be applied to plans and policies in the social world, but in doing this Popper is insistent that we begin not from some global or holistic blueprint for a good life, but from an observed and recognized problem. This is for two reasons. The first is that problems in the social world, such as infant hunger or teenage illiteracy or shortage of housing or poverty in the elderly, are not just easy to recognize. They will also be far more generally recognized to be problems and in need of attention, than will positive goals. Thus people from one perspective may advocate instant divorce and those from another will favour mothers staying at home, and another group will think that depressed people should be given the opportunity to end their lives, and so on. There will be no general consensus on such positive ideals, and *a fortiori* no agreement on what, if anything, should be done in relation to them. Popper thus favours what he calls negative utilitarianism: public policy should concentrate on solving problems where there is obvious suffering or harm. We are a very long way here from the type of revolutionary and wholesale slate cleaning advocated by Marxists and the like. Because any social policy will impact on individual people, in political policy large-scale revolutionary change should be eschewed in favour of what he calls piecemeal social engineering, small-scale measures whose effects can be monitored and controlled carefully and bit by bit. Here there is a contrast between Popper's view of science (in some ways the more radical the theory the better) and his view of social policy. But both can be seen as consequences of the demands of the critical approach in each case.

So, policies are then devised to deal with an agreed problem or ill in society. But, as we have already noted, no problem is without unsuspected and unintended consequences. An open society will be one in which genuine attempts are made to monitor the consequences of policies, and this will include taking seriously the reactions and experiences of those most affected by the policies. As these are often the least privileged, means should be found of taking their experiences and criticisms of a policy seriously. Popper's genuine humanitarianism shows itself here. And, as with science, so in social policy, Popper will be wary of remitting decision-making solely to accredited 'experts', whether these are civil servants, university academics or members of the professions involved in any area.

Popper insists that here, as in all other areas, the provenance of an idea is unimportant. What matters is its cogency, its genuineness and its testability. And the real test of a new policy will often be where it hits hardest, its effect on the least privileged. As opposed to the revolutionary holist, attempting to arrange society according to his blueprint, Popper refers to his approach to policy-making as piecemeal social engineering. If the term 'engineering' is perhaps not the happiest in this context, certainly the spirit behind it is both intellectually modest and humanly sensitive, sensitive to what matters to the people affected most both by the problems in question and the attempts to solve them.

Popper himself did not directly discuss what has come to be known as identitarian decision-making, that because one comes from a particular group, particularly a group that is seen as underprivileged, one's ideas or reactions to a situation have a special force or validity. With his stress on the individual qua individual, together with his dismissal of the importance of an idea's provenance, he would be hostile to any identitarian approach to policy, a reaction compounded by the fact that most people do not have a single identity in this sense. Certainly, Popper himself, a middle-class assimilated Jew from Vienna, who lived and worked for a time in New Zealand (and liked it) and eventually became a leading philosopher living contentedly in England, would have been hard to place in any single group identity, nor would he have wanted to have been.

One of the key themes in Popper's thinking about the open society is that most previous political philosophy, including notably Plato's, is focused on the question as to who should rule. For Popper, this is the wrong question and is comparatively unimportant compared to the key driver of openness. The open society will most likely be a democratic society, but as Popper knew from his experience of Germany and Austria in the 1930s, a democratic majority in itself is no guarantee of either openness or of individual freedom. Even if Hitler did not technically achieve a majority in 1933, he did use his democratic coalition to establish his dictatorship, and in 1938 in Austria he did achieve a massive majority following the Anschluss. In other words, democracy can itself be used to abolish democracy and to close down openness in a society. If democracy says that the people should rule, this is no guarantee that the majority of the people should not vote democratically to elect a totalitarian system in which there is no more democracy. (And 1930s Germany and Austria may not be the only instances of democracy turning or being turned in this way.)

For Popper the question is not who should rule, but whether a population can change its rulers, and how. The key driver of the open society is the ability of a people to get rid of its rulers regularly and peacefully, which, occasional blips aside, is the situation in Britain and the United States, and indeed in New Zealand, which Popper proclaimed to be the best and most easily governed society in the world. So the democracy which Popper supports is not a democracy which is rule by the people but a democracy in which the people are judges of the rulers. In such a situation the rulers will know that unless they keep the people content for the most part, they will lose power after four or five years of rule. Of course, this is not all that is required by openness. A truly open society will require institutions which promote openness, such as a free press, freedom of association, property rights, the rule of law, and so on, all of which tend to disappear in a closed society, if they ever existed in the first place. And for them to exist it is not enough for a notional existence of such institutions and practices in a constitution or legal system. Popper emphasizes that the open society requires not just right laws, even more, it requires that the people running the institutions of the society are imbued with the right mentality and motivation, keen to abide by the spirit of these institutions, and to protest if and when they feel they are being infringed.

An important, but often overlooked, aspect of an open society is the prominence within the society of traditions and traditional institutions. This point is connected to the importance of piecemeal social engineering, as opposed to wholesale revolutionary slate cleaning, the attempt to re-frame a society from the top down on some set of basic, usually abstract, principles. Not only would such an attempt be intellectually and morally hubristic. It would, because of the unpredictability of outcomes, be very likely to have large and unwelcome results. It would also deprive the populace of the framework of stability and stable expectations afforded by often unspoken traditions and by institutions which provide a framework for the conduct of life. Not everything can be taken into account at any one time. Traditions and institutions, along with the rule of law, provide a context in individuals can form reasonable and reasonably secure expectations as to how others, including authorities, will behave towards them, and equally how they will be expected to behave themselves. Anarchic and lawless societies will lack just these safeguards, to the detriment of everyone, including even a despotic ruling group, which is highly likely to fall out of power sooner or later.

Rationalists, as opposed to the Popperian critical rationalist, are likely to jib at Popper's attitude to tradition. However, they fail to take into account the unforseeability of radical policy change, and hence the need for piecemeal social engineering. They also fail to realize that, even within the limits of piecemeal reform, it is possible to modify and change a tradition or an institution where there is an obvious and pressing problem in its working. But it is important to appreciate that the reform will itself be against the background of other traditions and institutions, which are not for the moment being revised or reformed. Popper's critical rationalism is neither a rigid tribalism in this regard, nor does it work for revolutionary wholesale upheaval.

However, the effectiveness of an open society depends not just on traditions and institutions. It also depends on a populace which is attuned to the spirit inherent in openness. In several places Popper talks of the importance of people with the right spirit running the relevant institutions and countries with appropriate traditions, where, for example, flagrant breaches of the rule of law or of freedom of speech are likely to be met with general, almost instinctive, disfavour. It is no doubt significant, as already observed, that he speaks just of Britain, the United States and New Zealand as being examples of jurisdictions where this is largely the case, and no doubt we could instance others. But this still leaves a question as to what the Popperian advocate of the open society could say about the countries in many parts of the world where there are no such traditions, even if there is support among some for an open society with regular, peaceful changes of government, the rule of law, a free press and the rest.

Popper himself seems not to address this problem directly. The most that can be done at this stage is to point out that traditions of openness took a long time to embed themselves in the countries that have them, and also that wholesale reform is usually fraught with more dangers than benefits. So, looking at the dismal results of trying to install open or what might be called liberal-democratic societies in countries such as Iraq and Afghanistan, maybe we should look to Popper's other nostrum of piecemeal social engineering – that it is always better, as far as possible, to solve social and political problems by gradual reform in the desired direction, whose effects are then monitored and reacted to in a gradualist manner.

This will not satisfy the zealots, who will press for immediate and radical change, but, as Popper suggests at the start of his essay on a rational theory of tradition, this simply recapitulates the old dispute between Edmund Burke and the French revolutionaries of the 1790s.[35] The one advocated gradual change where desirable, and a polity which could engage the affections of its people, and the other a wholly rational order which would brook no dissent and slaughtered its opponents – for, of course, the best of rational reasons. The revolutionaries claimed reason on their side, even commandeering Notre Dame de Paris as a 'temple of reason'. If rationalism implies a system built on the best of rational abstraction, who can say they were wrong? But, by contrast, can Burke be claimed as a 'critical rationalist' in this dispute? Can Popper, who

---

[35] Popper (1963), 120–35, at 120.

strives to reconcile rationalism and traditionalism, be seen as tending to the side of Burke? At the very least it could be said that Burke advocated change where there were problems which needed solutions, and, even in the case of Ireland, fundamental change to the discriminatory laws against Catholics. He was not a Tory and never a diehard reactionary, though whether that makes him a critical rationalist we will leave others to decide.

Before leaving the open society we need to look at various paradoxes inherent in the liberal, democratic order, which is what, in a broad sense Popper is defending.[36] The first is the paradox of democracy, which we have already mentioned. This is when a democracy democratically decides to vote in a tyrant, as happened not just in Austria and Germany in the 1930s, or, more broadly itself behaved tyrannically as Athenian democracy did in its brutality towards the island of Melos in 416BC, to say nothing of its condemnation of Socrates a little later. The paradox of freedom is when there is too much freedom so that the weak are bullied and enslaved. The paradox of tolerance is when the violently intolerant are tolerated, and begin to advocate the use of fists or pistols, as opposed to argument. Directly or indirectly they undermine tolerance, either by provoking violence or by forcing an intolerant reaction on the part of the liberal state. The intolerant can then claim that liberal tolerance is in fact a fiction, and, like Marcuse in the 1960s, begin talking about 'repressive tolerance', so as to undermine liberal society or at least its pretension to uphold freedom. Nevertheless, the state may have a duty in certain circumstances to suppress those who place themselves outside the limits of tolerance.

In all these cases, Popper suggests that a truly open society will, as the context requires, legislate and even act at one level against freedom and tolerance and work against majority rule if it means the rule of the majority inclined to abolish democracy. The hope would be that tyranny could be combatted by the means at one's disposal, such as institutional safeguards, traditions of liberty and further elections. He puts it that 'we (i.e. defenders of the open society) demand a government that rules according to the principles of equalitarianism and protectionism; that tolerates all who are prepared to reciprocate, i.e. who are tolerant; that is controlled by, that is accountable to, the public. And we may add that some form of majority vote, together with institutions for keeping the public well informed, is the best, though not infallible, means of controlling such a government. (No infallible means exist.)'[37] No infallible means exist, indeed. The open society, where it exists is always vulnerable to dilution, subversion, and worse.

---

[36] See Popper (1966), vol. I, 245–6.   [37] Popper (1966), vol. I, 265–6.

In 1989, near the end of his life, Popper gave a lecture to the Liberales Forum at St Gallen in Switzerland. In it, he counselled that where we have it, we should recognize that 'we live in heaven', as he puts it, compared to most of history and to most of the world, even today. A first heaven, not the seventh or a perfect one, providing a context in which individuals are treated as free and with respect, able to direct their own lives for themselves. But this heaven needs nurturing and defending against those who fail to recognize their good fortune, and who would 'insult and defame our world'.[38]

Thus the open society is, in some ways, the scientific community writ large. It rests on the rule of law, where science rests on honest testing and criticism. It rests on individualism and entrepreneurship where science requires discovery and innovatory theorists. It rests on open discussion and debate, with the provenance of ideas irrelevant to their worth, just as science should encourage mavericks and even eccentrics. It is no coincidence that in the West growth of open societies has gone along with growth in scientific ideas and progress, and no coincidence that together science and the open society have made the past centuries in the West the most successful history has known. But also, and significantly, the very factors which have made the West successful, criticism and self-criticism, have also at times produced despair with its nature. Popper is certainly not against social criticism, but his valedictory warning against despair about the first heaven in which we live is surely timely. We should also remember that his social and political philosophy has at its core a vision of the individual person, making his or her own way through life in freedom and dignity, respectful of tradition up to a point, but never imprisoned in a collective dogma or ideology.

4 Popper's Later Philosophy: The Self and the Three Worlds

4.1 Preamble: Irrational Faith in Reason

A striking but unexpected aspect of Popper's thinking is his view that critical rationalism itself is without any rational foundation. His argument here is rather similar to his rejection of inductive justifications of induction. In giving a rational justification of rationality itself one would be assuming the very thing that has to be proved. And the same would apply more precisely to the critical rationalist (Popper) attempting to justify his adoption of critical rationalism on the grounds that it is what critical rationalism – his own favoured stance in intellectual and moral matters – demands. It would be a case of presupposing just what has to be proved or validated. Popper's way out of

---

[38] Popper (1997), 90.

this conundrum is basically to accept it as it stands, and to insist that his adoption of critical rationalism amounts to an irrational faith in reason.

Not surprisingly many of Popper's followers have jibbed at this, and have engaged in ever more arcane methods to show that faith in reason is not irrational. Without going into detail here I will simply record my view that none of these attempts is successful. Certainly, they do not really get to Popper's own underlying intuition that the adoption of an attitude of critical rationalism is first and foremost a matter of morality, of value. For those wedded to it, it underlies all one's other values. As such it is not supported by any other value. So in that sense to justify critical rationalism because it is an attitude which promotes tolerance, kindness, compassion, open-mindedness, the unity of mankind, and the rest would be to bring certain principles which stem from critical rationalism, which are among the moral consequences of the attitude, to justify the attitude itself.

That Popper's own adoption of critical rationalism is fundamentally a moral choice comes out clearly when he addresses the question in Chapter 24 of *The Open Society and Its Enemies*. There he states firmly that the choice between critical rationalism, irrational as it is at bottom, and other more blatant forms of irrationalism 'is not simply an intellectual affair, or a matter of taste. It is a moral decision'.[39] He then goes on to argue that critical rationalism treats people as individual human beings, whereas other irrationalisms, such as communism, fascism and various religions, tend to treat individuals as members of collectives. In these collectives, individuals submerge and sacrifice their individuality for the warmth of the tribe. As closed and un-self-critical these modern collectives contain within them the seeds of hostility and hatred towards other collectives, just as was the case with the earlier tribal societies.

While one may not want to call this commitment to critical rationalism *irrational*, what is important here is the manner in which Popper sees his thought, both on science and on politics as stemming not from scientific or political considerations alone, but as rooted a passionately held commitment both to the unity of humanity and to the value of each individual person as the individual he or she is, quite independent of any collective to which he or she might be seen to belong. As we have seen, it was this very strong instinct that undelay his break with the communists in 1919, and it is no doubt part of what he meant when in 1969 he spoke of himself as being religious, something deeper than reason.

In Chapter 24 of *The Open Society and Its Enemies*,[40] he says that we are nowadays faced with a stark choice between 'two kinds of faith', 'a faith in

---

[39] Popper (1966), vol. II, 232.   [40] Popper (1966), vol. II, 245–6.

reason and in human individuality and a faith in the mystical faculties of man by which he is united to a collective'. Faith in reason is what guides the scientific enterprise, in the knowledge that this enterprise can never reach a conclusion and will never be free from critical doubt. And while it can describe general laws operating in or on the world, it can never exhaustively account for the character and individuality of any single person. For any of us, it is this unique and inexplicable individuality we each have which makes life worth living. (And one can easily see how the Popperian approach to politics would follow a similar trajectory.) By contrast, the irrationalist, who despises or discounts reason, makes human individuality seem a burden, and seeks salvation in a collective, to which he or she subjects him or herself.

Examples from Popper's own time would, of course, be Marxism and fascism, but the same phenomenon is highly prevalent today in what we have called identitarianism when individuals who see their identity as one of victimization. As victims, they refuse to engage in critical discussion, because critical discussion is a weapon of the victimizing force by which they are being oppressed. One difficulty with this form of identitarianism is that in the modern world, there are very few people who have a single ethnic identity or heritage: certainly not Popper, an assimilated Viennese Jew, who lived happily for most of his life in the Anglosphere, in New Zealand and England. Nor the present author, who is of Irish, Scottish, English and Dutch-Jewish ancestry, and who sees himself in none of these terms, but rather as an individual making his way through an imperfect but largely benign United Kingdom. And I – and Popper – would say largely benign. Whatever crimes had been committed in the past by the British or English, we in Britain and the United States now live, in Popper's own words from 1989, 'in heaven, the first heaven, of course, not yet the seventh. Our heaven can be greatly improved; so we should no longer insult or defame our world, which is far the best there has ever been'.[41]

From my Irish perspective, with an ancestor displaced in the Great Famine of the 1840s, I can lament and condemn the cruelties and tyranny wreaked on that unhappy island from the other side of the Irish Sea. But, as a rational individual, I see no profit in stoking old bitternesses and keeping them warm. A cool recognition of what has happened is imperative from both sides, and where appropriate, remorse, repentance even, but so is an attitude of forgiveness; so beyond that basic honesty, what is needed is an attitude whereby parties to old conflicts look to see how, in the light of a mutually acknowledged past, each of them as individuals can move on into a better future together. Regarding oneself as part of a collective defined by a painful past of oppression, will simply make

---

[41] Popper (1997), 90.

any open future as a free individual impossible. Equally refusal on the part of the descendants of the oppressors to recognize and admit what happened even centuries ago will simply help to keep repressed feelings of oppression smouldering and reproducing themselves.

So, as Popper rightly says, the choice is between seeing oneself as an individual recognizing the unity of mankind or as existentially a member of the collective from which one is deriving one's identity against the rest, 'an attitude which divides men into friends and foes, into masters and slaves'. He goes on to speak of the universal humanism he is advocating as a 'faith which has proved itself in deeds and which has proved itself as well, perhaps, as any other creed'.[42] In saying this he is underlining his own distance from any formal religious position, which, despite his nod in favour of undogmatic religion, he tends to see in terms of the mysticism he is rejecting. One wonders how fair this is to Christianity at least, and to the development of the notion of the brotherhood of mankind. 'There is neither Jew nor Greek, there is neither slave nor free, there is neither male nor female; you are all one in Christ Jesus' (*Galatians*, 3. 28–9). Many would take this to be the source of the idea of the unity of mankind with which Popper is so enamoured, which is an idea not to be found in earlier Greek or Roman thinking or indeed in the Jewish notion of a chosen people. However, those who quote *Galatians* in this way do not usually add the next clause: 'And if you are Christ's, then you are Abraham's seed, and heirs according to the promise'. Nor do they usually discuss what is to become of those who are not even of Abraham's extended seed or who are not one in Christ Jesus. Popper himself may have had little sympathy with any of this, because, as a fully assimilated and religiously agnostic Jew, he was always an opponent of the state of Israel as a Jewish homeland. And he adds that, while the teaching of the fatherhood of God may contribute greatly to establishing the brotherhood of man, 'those who undermine man's faith in reason are unlikely to contribute much to this end'. This undermining of faith in reason may, of course, be unfair to much Christian thought and practice, or at least to the Thomist version of Christianity, but it would not be unfair to Kierkegaard, with whose thought the young Popper once flirted if somewhat ambivalently,[43] or indeed to the various moments in which Christians have dogmatically persecuted heretics and attempted to convert non-believers with force. We will simply close this discussion by underlining the intimate connection in Popper's thought between faith in reason and a commitment to the inestimable value of each human individual, as we turn to Popper's conception of the human person.

---

[42] Popper (1966), vol. II, 258.   [43] See Hacohen (2000), 15–16 and 83–4.

4.2 Life and the Self

Popper did not write comprehensively about the self until 1977 in *The Self and Its Brain*, a study co-authored with his long-standing friend and colleague the neuroscientist Sir John Eccles. However, he had made his view of the topic abundantly clear back in 1953, with a short article entitled 'Language and the Body-Mind Problem'.[44] There he rejects the view that physicalistic and psychological descriptions of human behaviour are two non-conflicting ways of describing the same reality, and adopts a Cartesian approach. He expands this to introduce the idea of four distinct functions of human language, which he categorises as the expressive, the signalling, the descriptive and the argumentative. The first three functions he derives from Karl Bühler, while the fourth – very much an aspect of critical rationalism – he adds himself. The first two functions could be achieved by a purely physical organism, even a mechanism such as a thermometer or a machine programmed to respond to certain stimuli. The higher functions assume intention on the part of the speaker, a wish to solve a problem, or to communicate. Hence we can see these functions, and particularly the fourth function, being fulfilled fully only if we are prepared to credit the communicating organism with intention and indeed with rationality. As Popper tartly puts it, 'we do not argue with a thermometer'.[45]

As to the familiar anti-Cartesian doubts as to whether physical and mental entities and states could interact, Popper simply retorts that such doubts rely on an outdated conception of causality according to which things of different natures cannot interact. In the penultimate section, he points out that in our speech and behaviour we humans are capable of being swayed by logical or mathematical or even musical relationships as much as by the physical objects around us. As consequence, 'if we act through being influenced by the grasp of an abstract relationship, we initiate various physical causal chains which have no sufficient *physical* causal antecedents. We are then 'first movers', or creators of a physical 'causal chain''.[46] This thought, filled out and expanded, comes to dominate his later philosophy.

Here we have to begin with Popper's ideas on life itself. Although an advocate of Darwinian evolution, Popper can only be described as agnostic on the origin of life, or indeed on the mechanisms which yield the mutations which become dominant in a species in its struggle for survival in a competitive environment, much of the competition being against its own con-specifics, specifically and murderously against the ones without the favourable mutation. For Popper Darwinian evolution is weak on the causes of mutations, being

---

[44] The 1953 article is referred to here as printed in Popper (1963), 293–8.
[45] Popper (1963), 297.   [46] Popper (1963), 298.

largely an account of why developments which turn out to be favourable are favoured. Indeed he sees Darwin's great theory in terms of problem solving by individuals with the structures and mentality with which they are endowed. Changes in the endowment are not explained by Darwin; only why the changes which get embedded in a species are so embedded. Importantly for Popper, included in an animal's endowment are not just its physical structure and bodily organs, but also the behavioural repertoire by which its problem-solving efforts are directed. Evolution for Popper is thus a theory of creatures actively striving, consciously or otherwise, to address problems. It is not a causal account of why it has the physical or behavioural propensities it has, except insofar as these have emerged in earlier attempts to solve problems.

What then of life itself? Darwin himself is largely silent on this question. His theory says only that where there is life there will be evolution in his terms, that is by environmental selection of mutations which themselves arise randomly. Much is made by Darwin of the way animal breeders and horticulturalists work to get the qualities they want in their flocks and plants, by interbreeding and hybridization. Nature is not a breeder or a horticulturalist, but Darwin suggests that we look at nature as if it is trying to act in this way; its appearance of intentionality is given by the way the environment works on random mutations within species, to produce longer necks, faster running, the ability to move around in dark caves by echo-location and the rest. The underlying tweaks and developments arise through random mutation, rather than through the plans and intentions of agents, human or otherwise, but the process produces results in ways similar to what is done by humans intent on improving biological kinds.

But the processes highlighted in the Darwinian account presuppose that living (i.e. self-replicating) forms are already reproducing themselves, and so passing on their genetic and behavioural traits. As Popper himself observes, why we and other living things exist remains a problem: 'the origin of life may have happened only once, and it may be essentially improbable, and if so it would not be subject to what we normally call explanation; for explanation in probabilistic terms is always an explanation that, under given conditions, an event is highly probable'.[47] He follows Jacques Monod in asserting that before life appeared on earth, the probability of its occurring was 'virtually zero'.[48] This is because of the immense complexity underlying the appearance of life, not just the highly complex genetic structure in any life-producing molecule, but also the need for it to be in a similarly highly complex soup of enzymes, for which there would be no anterior explanation. We have some idea of the minimum conditions of life, but virtually none of how these conditions could

---

[47] Popper and Eccles (1977), 555.   [48] Popper and Eccles (1977), 28 See also Monod (1970).

have come about all together at the right time. Popper concludes that 'much speaks in favour of the view that this event was unique'.[49] Thus, in his terms, life in our universe is an emergent property. Organic life is a step qualitatively beyond anything in the inorganic world from which it emerged, but we can say nothing helpful about exactly how it emerged, how the conditions required were present all together without prior reason or cause. Popper considers panpsychism, the idea that even inorganic matter is at some level alive and conscious, but dismisses the notion as having no explanatory power, at least in the present state of knowledge in which the life and mind in the inorganic realm have so far escaped detection. Panpsychism fails to avoid the problem of the emergence of consciousness, he says, and we would add that it fails to address the similar problem of the emergence of life.[50]

For, even when we have a world which includes living things, the vast majority, from primitive amoeba to delicate plants and colossal trees, are not in any normal or detectable sense conscious. So is consciousness itself an emergent property, emerging from the living, but not conscious world of plants? Popper says that it is, citing in support the everyday transition from virtually no consciousness at all in deep sleep to wide-awake consciousness during our daily lives. Interestingly part of the reason that Popper gives this example is to suggest that in the evolutionary story of consciousness, and indeed, of life itself, emergence into the new state is a gradual matter: 'there ought to be degrees of life and degrees of consciousness'.[51] He is convinced that animals with a fully developed central nervous system are conscious, just as human infants are, and may even have a sense of time, though, as we will see shortly, this is not a full consciousness of time and hence not a full consciousness.

So, on Popper's account, we have degrees of consciousness in our own lives (from sleep to waking), in the gradual development of children (from a general awareness and some sense of expectation or need to a fully human possession of memory and thought), and in the development of consciousness historically through species (from rudimentary awareness in some early forms of life to full-blown animal and then human consciousness). All this would strike any reasonably observant person not troubled by philosophical or scientific theorizing on the matter, as both sensible and probably true. It is the picture most of us have. It will be need to be accounted for in more recondite attempts to explain it away, but is too often simply dismissed in materialist thinking on the topic. So let us go along with Popper here, but caution, as he does, that this still leaves the origins and original glimmerings of consciousness unexplained.

---

[49] Popper and Eccles (1977), 29. [50] Popper and Eccles (1977), 71.
[51] Popper and Eccles (1977), 438.

This is 'indeed a miracle', Popper says, but in a way takes the sting out of the tail by adding that the emergence of consciousness historically 'may not be a greater miracle than that we can wake up in the morning and recreate full consciousness out of more or less nothing'.[52] This would have been Popper's response to today's so-called mysterians, philosophers, such as Colin McGinn, who want to speak of consciousness as a mystery (which is where others will invoke panpsychism, so as to mitigate the mystery). My answer and Popper's would be that the emergence of consciousness is not a mystery at all. As we all know as a matter of brute fact, it is something that happens countless times every day to beings with a certain type of nervous system, to ourselves (from sleep), to babies (from birth) and to countless animals of different species and types. Calling it a mystery obscures this utterly basic reality. Nevertheless, this reality does at some moment in the distant past involve qualitative emergence from a world with no conscious beings to one with one or just a few until our world in which consciousness is, on land at least, with a few exceptions, ubiquitous. Popper is surely right to see this as currently inexplicable on our current ways of understanding the material world and its propensities.

Although Popper sees consciousness in terms of an emergent and gradual development from unconscious life to the consciousness of creatures such as a modern-day dog or horse, there is for him a far more significant development from the merely conscious dog or horse to the adult human being possessed of self-consciousness. With full self-consciousness, we are able to think about the future and the past and to reason critically and self-critically. This qualitative jump Popper ascribes principally to our ability to acquire and use language. It is, though, important to underline that even at the stage of animal consciousness, Popper sees a creature's awareness of its surroundings in terms of attempting actively to solve problems and to act. He thus distances himself from the characteristically empiricist account of the consciousness of the world being a matter of passively receiving data through one's sense organs and then processing them in our mind to form a picture of the world. The world thus forever remains at one remove from our perception of it (which is what we find in Hume, e.g. and led to his unassaugable scepticism about the physical world and its objects, including people).

For Popper, the creature and we humans are always in a world and in direct contact with it. We actively seek to solve problems in it and theorize about it, which is how his view of the self and of consciousness links with his activist, problem-solving accounts of science and society. Like Wittgenstein, he sees the mind and our mental capacities as being rooted in extra-mental or physical

---

[52] Popper and Eccles (1977), 105.

activity, so the problems bequeathed us by Humean positivistic empiricism as to how we construct our picture of the external world, and how reliable that picture is, never occur. We are always in that world, acting in it and re-acting to it. Emphasizing the nature of consciousness, he states that the biological functions of our mind are closely related to mechanisms of control.[53] For Popper, the self is not just a blank canvas on to which perceptions are imprinted. From the start it is an agent interpreting the world and acting in it and on it.

Consciousness achieves its full incarnation only when it is self-consciousness. This is not just consciousness of what surrounds the subject at the moment of perception, but crucially the ability of the subject to be aware of itself, to connect the present moment with what preceded it in the past, to reflect on him or herself and his or her beliefs and values in the present, and to anticipate what is to come in the future. Reflecting on the future will also lead to consideration of death, specifically one's own death, which Popper sees as intrinsic to a fully self-conscious existence in the way it guides us and leads us to evaluate our behaviour. The realization of death, he says, is one of the great discoveries which led to full self-consciousness, from which it follows that until they have this capacity children are not fully self-conscious.[54] For all these capacities the possession and use of language are essential.

Popper does not deny that tool-making is an important aspect of human life and culture. Indeed it is often, if controversially, taken to be a key indicator of intelligence not only in human beings but also in some other species. However, as he points out, language differs from tool-making in that it is clearly genetically based: 'the only tool that seems to have a genetic base is language'.[55] All human beings have language, though there are many different languages. Nevertheless, all the different languages are made possible by genetically based needs, capabilities and aims, which are the same in all human tribes and no doubt rooted in our brains and nervous systems. If Chomsky and his followers are correct, they are also based in specific mental grammatical structures common to us all, whatever language we speak.

But, over and above universal brain structure, learning a language is a considerable and specific cultural and intellectual achievement. According to Popper, it requires years of active work, some pleasurable, some painful, as one enters and begins to use the language of one's specific culture. A baby when born is not responsible for its actions, nor is it conscious of its numerical identity over time – two of Kant's key criteria for personhood. In learning a language the child extends his or her mastery over the material environment by discriminating the

---

[53] See Popper and Eccles (1977), 114. [54] Popper and Eccles (1977), 554.
[55] Popper and Eccles (1977), 48.

things he or she is aware of by means of linguistic classifications. He or she also very early acquires the crucial ability to interact with other people. The child learns to name the parts of his or her body and to use personal pronouns, thus gradually becoming self-conscious. Language, by hypostasizing objects, events, thoughts and memories, also allows the speaker to evaluate and plan and to examine what one thinks and values in a critical way. It is language which gives us our concept of time, of the past and the future, which is a key aspect of self-consciousness and of one's awareness of one's own ultimate end in death. Thus over time the developing person begins to assume responsibility and also a sense of his or her identity over time.

Significantly on self-consciousness, that is the awareness of myself as 'I', Popper takes issue both with Descartes and Kant.[56] Descartes makes the Cogito, the 'I think' the *fundamentum inconcussum* of all his philosophy and Kant speaks of a somewhat illusive 'I think' accompanying all our perceptions. Popper insists that the Cartesian thought 'I think, therefore I am' itself presupposes knowledge of the language (of the meanings of 'I' and 'am' and 'think' and 'therefore'), while against Kant he questions whether any idea of the self or ego accompanies all our experiences (as opposed to those in which we turn our mind that way). In both these observations Popper seems to me to have a better case than his opponents, one which simply underlines his basic sense that from the start thought and self-consciousness are embedded in action and speaking a language. (Interestingly Wittgenstein, his supposed philosophical antagonist, would have agreed with him on this crucial point.)

Thus the self-conscious self is not a passive receiver of sensations, but nor is it passive with regard to the body and the brain to which it is connected. Here Popper emerges as a fully committed dualist. The self pilots the brain, and hence the rest of the body through the brain. We (or, more correctly from his point of view, our self) 'feel that we are sitting in the driver's seat of our car, as it were', knowing part but not all of what we are doing, and what movements and actions we thus initiate. This driver-car picture can, he says, be taken as 'a model of the way in which the self interacts with the brain'.[57]

There is top-down causation in our own make-up, as the self decides what to do, and causes the body and limbs to do what we decide. Many philosophers will at this point argue that any such suggestion would be prevented by the closed causal structure of the physical world of which we are a part. To this Popper offers a dual response. Emergence in the biological and animal realms will also imply top-down causation. The behaviour of plants and animals is partially directed by the complexes of physical molecules that make up the

---

[56] See Popper and Eccles (1977), 49–50. [57] Popper and Eccles (1977), 486.

organism in question, directing it to operate in ways which could not be accounted for by analysis of the inorganic parts making up these complexes on their own. They act as they do only they are brought together so as to give the whole organism capabilities the molecules in question would not have if they were not in the system they are in.

Popper is also quite happy to say that the immaterial conscious self acts on its material brain. Assuming that consciousness is not material in the sense that the neurones in my brain are, many would jib at this. How can a non-material entity act on the clearly material stuff in my brain? Does not this clash with the hard ontology of materialistic physics?

Popper's view here is that the idea that stuff, material stuff, can be affected only by substances of a similar sort is well outdated. Indeed Hume himself argued that while causation involves constant conjunction between a cause and an effect, this does not that this implied any identity of constitution between the two. Popper develops this point by emphasizing that modern physics is far from working with the Cartesian notion of physical action and causation being a matter of action by the brute physical contact of pushes and pulls. Newton's gravitational force had already suggested that this was not so (to Newton's own puzzlement). Today as well as gravity there is a plurality of forces, including electrical, nuclear and weak forces, and fields of force through which the action of one body can affect another body distant from it.

In our case, what initiates a free action will be the self causing our brain and body to do things it is freely willing. As far as free action in a material world is concerned, many will point out that modern physics is indeterministic, which we have already seen Popper arguing for on grounds other than quantum indeterminacy. However, the appeal to quantum indeterminacy at this point is not immediately helpful. Free action is not a matter of chance. Quantum fluctuations do not themselves easily or clearly translate into actions which are observable at the macroscopic level. Nevertheless Popper concedes that it might be possible that they do, or at least that they give a kind of release from deterministic processes at the level of consciousness. The self, through what it wants, might act on fluctuations in the brain to produce the intended action. In other words, quantum indeterminacy might provide a physical space within which the conscious self can communicate and effect its choices.[58]

Would the idea of a self-acting in this sort of way interfere with the second law of thermodynamics, as some have alleged? Popper says that the brain will heat up during some intense mental activity at the conscious level, and then tire – as we all know from experience. This heating up and consequent

---

[58] See Popper and Eccles (1977), 541.

degradation of energy in the brain at the physical level will to some extent preserve the second law. In any case, we already know that in the case of Brownian motion that law is violated in the small, a violation 'amply compensated for by what happens in neighbouring parts of the system'.[59] The first law of thermodynamics, that postulating a conservation of energy in a way elicits a more interesting response from Popper from our point of view. He takes the analogy of a vessel being steered from inside, which violates no physical law.[60] This is because it changes direction by using energy inside itself to push an equal amount of mass (in this case water) outside itself. In the case of our own actions, we know that a very small touch can at times produce a disproportionately large result, such as a light finger touch on an electric organ producing a deafening sound. So very little energy, perhaps an almost negligible amount, will have to be expended for the self to act on the brain, 'yet the brain may still be "open"; to the self and the self may be working on it'.[61]

In all of this, we are working on the boundaries of what we know or what science currently tells us. Popper suggests that we should not worry too much about possible slight violations of the law of the conservation of energy, or about any other similar anomalies. Because of the degree of corroboration in observation and experiment, we should accept that our present physics is valid as a first approximation. But, from the paradoxes of quantum theory, from the lack of a grand theory uniting quantum theory and relativity, and also from the increasingly baroque speculations in cosmology about possible worlds and antimatter, we know that our present physics is beset with problems. In Popper's own words, 'I myself hope for a revolution in physics because I feel that the present state of physics is unsatisfactory'.[62] Like Einstein, he was always unhappy with quantum theory generally. His admiration for Bohr and the Copenhagen theorists notwithstanding, he used to quote the sentry Marcellus in Shakespeare's *Hamlet* to the effect that 'something is rotten in the state of Denmark'.

Popper's hope for a revolution in physics is all of a piece with his antiessentialism in science, or indeed in any other field. Our theories, however successful, are, like Newton's, always provisional, and they should be regarded as such. As we saw earlier in connexion with Popper's anti-essentialism in science, our fundamental explanatory concepts and theories are never really fundamental, and may be revised or even revolutionized in the future. Nevertheless what they are tested against has ultimately to be what is given to us in everyday experience, which is the point from which we live and act, and

---

[59] Popper and Eccles (1977), 543. [60] See Popper and Eccles (1977), 180.
[61] Popper and Eccles (1977), 565. [62] Popper and Eccles (1977), 543.

will furnish what philosophers refer to as the empirical basis of our theorizing. Bohr himself took this to mean that the concepts of classical Newtonian science were also methodologically fundamental, as deriving clearly from that empirical experience. How far Popper would agree with this is not altogether clear, but what is clear is how the empirical basis works in relation to the self and theorizing about the mind: 'to assume that Michelangelo's works are simply the results of molecular movements and nothing else seems to me very much more absurd than the assumption of some slight and probably unmeasurable violation of the first law of thermodynamics'.[63] Thus any scientific theory of the mind, brain or experience, however recondite, is absurd if it denies what we all, before being seduced by that theory, know about the titanically inventive and creative Michelangelo and his works, and indeed about our own faltering activity as free, rooted in our conscious experience, and subject to praise or criticism as the case may be. We should reject the theory and not fuss philosophically about the basic experiential reality.

4.3 Popper's Three Worlds

We have already seen that Popper makes the use and possession of language the basis for human self-consciousness. To use Bühler's schema as modified by Popper, it is language which allows us to describe and argue where non-linguistic animals can only express their immediate feelings and signal to others about the environment as it is at the time of the signal. Language allows us to describe the world and our own state according to shared conventions and beyond what is given to us in the present moment, and, crucially for Popper, to assess and criticize those descriptions. A human language is not simply the sounds we make in using it or the marks we make in writing down bits of speech. It is the abstract system in which those sounds and marks have the meaning they do, allowing us to convey our thoughts to others and beyond what we might want to express or signal in response to some immediate stimulus. Writing is hugely significant here, allowing the thoughts of one person or people at one time to become available for use and scrutiny by others, in times and at places removed from the original place of utterance.

It is the abstract system behind the words and inscriptions which affords the physical speech and writing their significance, which includes expressing and understanding new sentences and thoughts. In so doing, as well as understanding the language of others, we will be conscious of what we are intending to say, and in saying or writing what we mean we will be using physical sounds or marks. As physical objects words and inscriptions are just bits of movement in

---

[63] Popper and Eccles (1977), 544.

wavelengths or ink marks on paper, produced by other movements in the atmosphere or by drops of ink from pens or the clattering of keys in printers. All this is inherently without meaning, unless and until looked at in terms of the abstract grammatical and semantic structurers the physical marks and sounds embody, which, as linguists tell us, go to make a language a means of communication and of the transmission of ideas. It is language conceived in terms of its non-physical structures and meanings that make it so important in the development of a child's self-consciousness.

In this story there are three levels. At the most basic level, we have the sounds or marks on paper, physical stuff. This particular physical stuff is produced by conscious human beings, who operate in this area with intention and knowledge, which is our second level, the level of human consciousness. But in using language the conscious person is working with an abstract system, which allows meanings to be conveyed through physical sound or marks. And the meanings which can be conveyed are endless in scope and number. Each one of us language users has the ability to say and think things that have never been said or thought before, but which will be understood by other speakers of the same language by virtue of his or her grasp of the language as an abstract and ever developing structure.

Here in a nutshell we have an outline of Popper's three worlds theory. The three worlds are World 1, the physical world, dumb and meaningless, and going on according to the laws of nature; World 2, the world of consciousness, including human consciousness, and so the world in which our feeling, thinking, intending, self-reflecting, hoping, fearing, and so on takes place; and World 3, the world of the products of the human mind, including mathematics, stories, explanatory myths, tools, scientific theories, social institutions and works of art[64]; and also artistic styles and traditions, languages conceived as structures of meaning, and much else besides. These are the frameworks by which much of our World 2 activity is governed and directed, and to which we respond in what we do. Our World 2 mental activity has its effect on World 1, through our self interacting with the brain and the physical world via its intentions and activity. But World 1 also impacts on World 2 (us) with the problems it sets us. So as well as us being influenced by World 3, so we influence and change it, by what we think about its set-ups and structures. Thus the three worlds are connected and influence each other in an unending cycle of mutual interaction.

Although we have taken language as the way into World 3, Popper's own starting point is mathematics. He thinks that mathematics, like all the other denizens of World 3, is in its origins a human invention. Presumably at some

---

[64] See Popper and Eccles (1977), 34.

early stage of human existence a group of hunter-gatherers began counting their animals, one, two, three and so on, up to a fairly low number given the size of the herd and what it is possible to scrutinize physically, so as to check on the herd when it was loose on the savannah, or to know whether some other group had stolen one, and for similar practical purposes. After a while the counters would think of the signs they were using for this purpose, the numbers in other words, as a system in their own right, which could be used for calculating the quantities of any type of object. Thus, in this, or in some similar process of measuring quantities, arithmetic had been invented.

Popper is not particularly interested in the process of invention – the counting story I have just given is mine rather than his. What is crucial for Popper is that once the system of arithmetic has come into existence, in whatever human activity actually led to it, it begins to take on a life of its own, with extensions way beyond the original use. For Popper the autonomous development of a World 3 object once it has been created is absolutely crucial. Like a spider's web, it will continue with a life of its own after its creator has gone and with uses and developments unsuspected by its creator. Accordingly, in his earliest developments of the theory he speaks of World 3 knowledge as 'objective', that is, not in anyone's mind, or as epistemology without a knowing subject.[65]

To give a simple, but nonetheless significant example of World 3 objectivity and autonomy, once numbers had been invented it would be true that there is an infinity of numbers. A simple proof assures us that to any highest number we have, it is always possible to add one more, without end. This insight leads to the idea that there is an infinity of numbers. I will leave aside here the question as to whether there is a completed infinity or whether infinity refers to the unending sequence. Most mathematicians, will opt for the completed infinity, which is regarded as necessary for most systems of mathematics. But either way, infinity is beyond our powers of counting or grasping. Yet it is a consequence, a real and true consequence, of our primitive herdsman fumbling his way to twelve. Once the number is invented, infinity follows, even though it is way beyond what was originally envisaged. It remains beyond our powers fully to envisage or comprehend. But it is real and its existence is true.

And so with many other remarkable mathematical results, such as Goldbach's conjecture or Fermat's last theorem. Goldbach's conjecture, that every even number is the sum of two primes has been shown to be true for every case that has been examined, but so far, since Goldbach conjectured it in 1742, there is no proof that this is universally true. Yet if it is true, its truth will not suddenly spring up if and when a proof is discovered. If true, it is true now, and always

---

[65] Popper (1978), Ch3 and Ch4, 106–90.

was, at least since human beings started calculating. Fermat's last theorem is particularly apt for Popper's purpose, because when Fermat proposed his result in 1637 he provided no proof. This was not forthcoming until 1993 when Andrew Wiles finally announced a proof, some 350 years after Fermat. Yet the theorem was still true even before the proof had been discovered, as we now know, given that it has been proved. The truth of the theorem did not magically spring up only when the proof arrived, for there is a sense in which mathematical truths are timeless. Similarly, once numbers had been invented, some numbers were prime, which presumably did not emerge into human consciousness until much later. We were told in 2024 that the largest prime number so far known has 41,024,320 digits, and this was discovered using a cloud-based computer, so way beyond the calculating power of a mere human with paper and pencil. But whatever the number is, it was always prime, and its existence and the truth about its primehood follow once numbers themselves are in existence. Indeed neither the notion of prime nor its recognition in a particular case are conceptually difficult: both follow from simple definitions. Even if the first mathematicians, if we may so call them, only counted up to 12, and lacked the concept of primehood, 1, 3, 5 and 7 were prime, as were 13, 17, 19 and so on, even beyond their knowledge, and on and on endlessly, even beyond today's extraordinary number.

What Popper is proposing for mathematics is a type of Platonism. That is, he is insisting that mathematics contains truths we may not recognize and which may transcend our grasp or ability to prove, which is certainly part of what Platonists, including Plato himself, hold. A further important motivation for mathematical Platonism is that mathematical objects and truths are abstract, and hence timeless. Popper would go along with this up to a point. Indeed he actually maintains that as we have no finite physical model of a potential infinity, a purely materialistic mathematics would be finitistic, and hence severely restricted.[66] But on the abstractness of mathematics, there is a significant difference between Popper and Platonism in the traditional sense. Platonic timelessness implies eternity in the objects in question and existence in a perfect and transcendent world of Forms, which are more real than the lower existences here on Earth. There is no sense in Plato that any of the objects in the Platonic perfect realm, which include far more than numbers, have a history or are human inventions. Whereas, as we have seen, Popper holds that mathematical objects are human inventions, even if, once invented they project truths unknown to us, which may exceed our grasp. Not only are Popper's World 3 objects human inventions, but Popper's sense of religion leaves him agnostic

---

[66] See Popper and Eccles (1977), 550.

over God. He actually expresses an antipathy to life after death,[67] and will have no truck with any Platonic heaven in which eternal Forms exist.

Popper's World 3 may make more sense when applied to its non-mathematical denizens. For anyone in the slightest degree tempted by mathematical Platonism, it is hard to see how numbers and theorems could spring into existence *en masse* and beyond anyone's ken only after humanity's first fumbling efforts at counting animals and the like. But when it comes to the other products of human culture which Popper places in World 3, such as language, political and social institutions, science itself considered as a human endeavour, artistic styles and traditions, Popper's combining of the human invention with abstract systems of meaning which have unknown consequences, may well be easier to accept than any full-bloodied Platonism. Morality and value could be a borderline case between Platonism in the traditional sense and Popper's World 3 Platonism. But if we think that moral values can both be objective and at the same time be responsive to the specific conditions of human nature in a world of our type, Popper's combining of objectivity and brute historical contingency is attractive. Once a world such as ours comes into existence with beings such as ourselves in it, certain values will obtain, objectively and apart from our choices, but just because we and our world are as they are.

We have already looked at language as having dimensions of physicality and systematic structures of abstract meaningfulness. Its indefinite expansiveness beyond the conceptions or intentions of its originators and its current users is a further key element of its nature as a World 3 object. We can fruitfully apply a similar analysis to works of art and to the traditions within which they are produced.

A poem, such as Tennyson's *Ulysses* is obviously a collection of sounds in the air, if recited out loud, or a lot of marks on paper if printed in a book. These World 1 phenomena will have their analyses as physical objects, but they only come to life when they are uttered or perceived by conscious and self-conscious beings, such as Tennyson himself or his listeners or readers. These World 2 elements are not merely aspects of animal consciousness. A dog or a horse might be conscious of someone producing the World 1 sounds. But it will only be a human being, clued into the poem's World 3 aspects who will actually understand the poem as a poem. They will first have to understand the English language as the World 3 system of grammar and semantics, and at a sophisticated level. They will then be able to understand the bare meaning of the poem, but only its bare meaning. To get what Tennyson expects the reader to understand they will first have to understand that the bare rock referred to in

---

[67] See Popper and Eccles (1977), 556.

the first section is the Ithaka to which Ulysses (=Odysseus) is returning, and then the Trojan War, his odyssey, the circumstances of his return and the reason why he sets off again, and where. Homer's *Iliad* and *Odyssey* will have to be part of the context for anyone who understands the poem with any degree of sensitivity, and also, I suggest, Dante's moving account of Ulysses' ultimate voyage in *Inferno*. Then the sensitive reader will also have to make up his or her mind as to whether the effects Tennyson contrives are both well conveyed and well-judged, or not, and how.

Tennyson would have expected his readers to have his references to Homer and Dante up their sleeves, which is why the poem will be all but incomprehensible to the average reader in the twenty-first century. This simply underlines the importance in appreciating an apparently straightforward poem of its grounding in World 3 traditions and contents. Tennyson was part of a two-and-a-half millennia World 3 tradition and he developed that tradition in ways unsuspected by either Homer or the classical Greeks more generally or by Dante. Thinking of *Ulysses* in this way gives a good idea of how Popper's World 3 might work in human culture, informing and vivifying its works both for its creators and its recipients; indeed a perceptive reader might see things in the poem beyond Tennyson's own World 2 thoughts and intentions. What Popper will emphasize here is the way in which the World 3 aspects of *Ulysses* are distinguishable from either its World 1 materiality or its World 2 creation and reception. All three worlds are necessary, and play their parts, as the material basis, the conscious reception and the cultural meaning and context. What Popper continually emphasizes is the way that the World 3 contribution is behind the World 1 and 2 inputs, and will go beyond them, even way beyond.

Clearly, as Popper sets his picture up, World 3 has to be regarded as neither material nor conscious, in the same way that the meaning of this sentence is immaterial. The meaning is embodied in physical sounds or marks, but with an abstract World 3 content. Its meaning would be the same in different words, in different languages and even if only thought in some sort of mental shorthand. But, as self-conscious human beings, with language and thought based on our linguistic capabilities, we are open to the content of World 3, and we are influenced by it in our conscious and indeed our physical activity. And, this content is extensive. We have looked briefly at language and poetry, but similar analyses can be given of all the significant aspects of human life, whether they be political institutions, manners, morality, cultural forms, artistic traditions, sporting activity, religious practice and much else beside. In all we are open to the immaterial dimensions of the significance of cultural productions. We are influenced by them, conscious of them, influencing them in our turn, and yet also transcended by them, in the way that even what we do ourselves will have consequences and meanings beyond those of which we are conscious.

As we saw in our analysis of the poem, unless we are steeped in the traditions underlying a strand of our cultural life, that strand will wither, to our disbenefit. As we saw in the opening of our earlier section on historicism, Popper himself believed that just this had happened in the case of musical and artistic tradition, with a general decline in the result. Popper's insistence in his analysis of World 3 on the significance of tradition for a culture connects here with his earlier demolition of historicism. The disparagement of tradition and its methods which plays so large a role in artistic life today is, in Popper's view, directly attributable to the fact that those involved in the arts 'listen to bad prophets, bad philosophers', who profess to know the way the future is going. Instead of 'trying to create good work, they (artists and musicians) concentrate on becoming leaders for the future'.[68] But, as we know from Popper's earlier work, no one is in a position to anticipate the future. Historicism dominates in the arts these days, as Popper knew from personal experience in Vienna with Schoenberg in music and no doubt with the work of Adolf Loos and the other architects of the time too. Dare one comment that in 2025 the Viennese modernists of the early twentieth-century look benign compared to the decadence and anarchy which now obtains in the most prestigious artistic institutions? The Viennese modernists might look benign today, but their insistence on art starting afresh without regard to the long tradition of the previous millennium remains, in mutated form, dominant today. Popper's analysis is still pertinent.

To end this overview of Popper's late views on the self and World 3 we are left with a puzzle. Popper believes in an immaterial self and in a non-material world 3, in a symbiotic relation to each other, each receiving its sustenance and life from the other. World 3 and all its facets make the self what it is – not essentially material even where embodied in material form, not merely conscious; World 3 is a continuous creation by selves, beings in World 2 that is, even where it transcends what it has been given by these World 2 selves. This picture looks compelling and fruitful, particularly in the way that it treats of the functions and relationships of the three worlds. There are certainly Platonic resonances in it, particularly in the quasi-autonomous nature of World 3 when it comes to mathematics and the development of institutions and styles.

And yet. Popper is not a Platonist. World 3, even in its autonomous development once it is created, remains a human creation. And the human selves that create it are emergent from earlier, more primitive forms of life, rather than descended from a higher level of existence, as Plato would have it. Where Plato

---

[68] See Popper (1997), 41.

has his process being governed by a transcendent One, a combination of truth, beauty and goodness, Popper has nothing to offer. Where do we come from? Where are we going? Popper simply leaves us with big questions regarding as to the provenance of the selves and direction and locus of World 3. It is as if Popper sees the need for these quasi-Platonic realities, persuasively in my view. This puts him at odds with mainstream philosophical and scientific opinion, but he has nothing to offer as to how these realities come about, beyond an appeal to emergence about which he himself admits it is hard to say anything.[69] The appeal *explains* very little. In my concluding section, I will offer a few thoughts on this predicament in the light of Popper's earlier views on science and society.

5 Conclusion: Popper's Vision

Popper sees the story of science since the sixteenth century as one of progress by means of the critical-empirical approach adopted by figures such as Galileo and Kepler, and later Newton and a host of other great scientists and thinkers. The critical rationalism admired by Popper may have had its roots in classical Greece, but its empirical application as expressed in his demarcation criterion really took root only in Europe since the sixteenth century, though now it is to all intents and purposes universal, having spread all over the world in a culture neutral way. Scientific truth, due to nature rather than us, is no respecter of language or culture. Progress there certainly has been, but in Popper's view it has been through a somewhat jagged story of critical testing, refutation of preceding theories and formulation of new theories to deal with past problems. In his view, this process is not guaranteed to succeed indefinitely; certainly, we will never be able to say that we have found the final truth, if such a thing is even conceivable. He looks for a revolution in science, but with little sense of what this might amount to. Further his criticism of induction indicates that we will never be able predict what scientific or other problems we will face in the future.

In is social and political thinking Popper advocates open as opposed to closed societies. As with science, there has been astonishing progress in this regard in the jurisdictions which aspire to openness. He is admiring particularly of the open societies of the Anglosphere, though not uncritical of their defects. Once again he will look to a process of continual criticism and of genuine attempts to solve manifest problems in a spirit of openness. And once again the process will be unending with progress by no means guaranteed against countervailing tendencies and temptations. Moreover, against historicists, even those who see history moving in a liberal-democratic open spirit, there is no direction to history, at least none that we are in a position to foresee. Popper's anti-inductivism operates in the

---

[69] See Popper and Eccles (1977), 29.

social sphere too. And human beings are, or should be, free, unpredictable individuals, who will benefit from the ability to exercise that freedom, and so will the societies in which they live. The contrast between the West and the rest, including the communist rest, in that respect hardly needs underlining.

The title of Popper's intellectual autobiography is *Unended Quest* which captures much of the spirit of his work, as does the title of the earlier collection *Conjectures and Refutations*. But beneath all this questing and testing, and stress on critical rationalism, what we find is an irrational faith, as we have seen. And the faith is not only irrational. The anti-inductivist doubts about future progress either in science or in society undercut any hope one might look for in Popperian faith, even as that faith inspires us to go on plumbing the mysteries via conjecture and refutation.

To some extent the introduction of a free immaterial self and of an abstract, relatively time-free World 3 mitigates some of these doubts, though it raises other questions. As already emphasized both are a welcome contrast to the materialistic physicalism of much contemporary thought. Both reflect key aspects of lived experience which are absent from or simply ignored in that thinking. They suggest a richer ontology, a world and an existence not confined to the limits of contemporary physics or philosophy or to the lives of any individual. Appeal to this richer ontology is reinforced by Popper's frequent references to the surpassing greatness of figures such as Michelangelo and Bach, Mozart, Beethoven and Schubert, and to his long friendship with the distinguished pianist Rudolf Serkin. These people all lived lives and created works way beyond the everyday, intimating higher values and other levels of existence.

Relevant at this point is the mutual admiration between Popper and Sir Alister Hardy, the well-known zoologist who went on to found the Religious Experience Research Unit in the University of Oxford. Hardy wrote of the surprise and delight he felt in 1965 in receiving from Popper a copy of his lecture 'Of Clouds and Clocks' (a strong analysis and defence of human freedom and rationality). Popper himself praised Hardy's 'important contribution' to the history or organic evolution in the latter's *Living Stream*, a 'great book', according to Popper, for which he had 'the greatest admiration', in which Hardy spells out the relation of the theory of evolution to the spirit of man.[70]

Hardy was, naturally, an evolutionist and an admirer of Darwin. But he was also an admirer of Alfred Russel Wallace, Darwin's co-founder of the theory of evolution, but who departed from Darwin over the special nature of human beings and their destiny. Wallace was a firm believer in natural selection in the

---

[70] Hardy (1984), 22; Popper and Eccles (1977), 12–13.

animal kingdom, firmer indeed than Darwin himself, but held that 'there is a difference in kind, intellectually and morally, between man and other animals; and that while his body was undoubtedly developed by the continuous modification of some ancestral animal form, some different agency, analogous to that which first produced organic *life*, and then originated *consciousness*, came into play in order to develop the higher intellectual and spiritual nature of man'.[71]

Hardy himself took his lead from Wallace, and went on to speculate that what Wallace called our spiritual nature means that we humans are or can be in touch with a divinity above and beyond the world in which we live. Hence his interest in religious experience, and especially those experiences where people have felt some prayer or aspiration being answered from above. Popper would clearly not go along with that, and probably not with Wallace's talk of our *spiritual* nature. However, and replacing the notion of agency with that of emergence, the passage just quoted from Wallace presents a picture of the animal and human evolution remarkably similar to Popper's. Both hold that there are qualitative differences between inorganic, organic, animal and human life. And, although Popper might not like Wallace's 'spiritual', he is, as we have already emphasised a thorough-going dualist when it comes to humanity. He also, as we saw earlier, wanted to talk of all men, himself included as religious. But religious only in a certain sense, namely as believers in mystery and influenced by a reality which transcends us and inspired by the desire to find out more, and also by a duty to be compassionate to one another. But not religious in any traditional sense, or with a belief in a transcendent personal God behind the mysteries. The real difference between Wallace and Hardy on the one hand, and Popper on the other, lies not in the description and analysis of the processes leading to human nature or indeed on the special capacities of that nature, but in the suggestion that there might be a cosmic creator or plan underlying those processes, and one to which or whom our destiny is directed.

Popper's vision is not just of immaterial selves and human products entering a World 3 that is rooted in World 1 and conceptualized in World 2, but is not part of either of them. It is also a vision of extraordinary findings in science through human beings employing both their ingenuity and their critical reason and of polities of security, law and freedom, again through the deployment of the critically directed machineries of openness. Taking all the parts together, this is a vision of a world so far from the pre-human organic and inorganic realm from which it emerges that it naturally provokes thoughts of a higher form of existence altogether. Such thoughts, of course, inspired thinkers such as Plato and Descartes, who without demur immediately begin to think of another world

---

[71] Wallace (1905), 17; quoted in Hardy (1984), 76–7.

more perfect than ours, to which we in this world are drawn. In a different modality thinkers such as Hardy, Bergson and Teilhard de Chardin (to whom Hardy refers respectfully) would see our world, as described by Popper and himself, as a step in a cosmic process to greater spirituality, knowledge and perfection.

Such a move would also incidentally provide the beginnings of an answer to Popper's scepticism about induction, and possibly also about progress in whatever sphere. If we are part of a cosmic process moving towards greater perfection in various fields, then it would be reasonable to see our understanding of our world as increasing and improving, albeit jaggedly and through revolutions and upheavals in our theories and explanations, as we become more attuned to it. On this view, we humans, critically rationalist humans, are the means by which the inorganic and non-linguistic world becomes articulate about its nature, and also the means by which more open and truly human forms of living can be brought about.

Popper, of course, would resist any such move towards a cosmic destiny or purpose for our kind. Not only is his rejection of induction implacable, but he also repudiates of any idea of a pre-determined direction of history. These positions are reinforced by his coolness towards the possibility of immortality in a next world and his reluctance to speculate any further about the transcendence of World 3 beyond the mere fact that there is such a thing.[72] Popper's reticence here leaves his vision both excitingly suggestive and tantalizingly incomplete.

I am going to add no more at this point. I would not presume to say what Popper might or might not have thought had he lived longer and pursued his thinking about the self and World 3 further, or indeed on what I might think he should have said. Nor do I think that invoking divine or other agencies in the story necessarily or easily gives us more understanding of the processes involved than does Popperian invocation of emergence. In conclusion, I will confine myself to saying that the self and World 3 would fit seamlessly into a Hardyesque or even a Platonic picture, as embodying a spiritual dimension of our existence. But this just where Popper, perhaps wisely, chose to be silent.

---

[72] See the discussions in Popper and Eccles (1977), 556 and 563.

About the Author

Anthony O'Hear, OBE, Profesor of Philosophy, University of Buckingham. From 1994 to 2019, he was Director of The Royal Institute of Philosophy, and Editor of its journal 'Philosophy'. Among his publications are 'Karl Popper' (1980); 'Beyond Evolution: Human Nature and the Limits of Evolutionary Explanation' (1997); 'After Progress' (2000); (with Natasha O'Hear) 'Picturing the Apocalypse: The Book of Revelation in the Arts over Two Milllennia' (2015); 'Transcendence, Creation and Incarnation' (2020); 'The Prism of Truth: Reflections on Myth' (2024). He has advised several British governments on education over a number of years.

References

Charlton, W. (2019), 'Saying and Signifying', *Philosophy 94*, 3–25.
Darwin, F. (ed.), (1903), *More Letters of Charles Darwin, Vol II*, London: John Murray.
Fukuyama, F. (1992), *The End of History and the Last Man*, New York: Free Press.
Hacohen, M. (2000), *Karl Popper: The Formative Years 1902–1945*, Cambridge: Cambridge University Press.
Hardy, A. (1965), *The Living Stream*, London: Collins.
Hardy, A. (1984), *Darwin and the Spirit of Man*, London: Collins.
Havel, V. (1986), *Living in Truth*, London: Faber and Faber.
Kolnai, A. (1938), *The War against the West*, London: Victor Gollancz.
Kuhn, T. (1962), *The Structure of Scientific Revolutions*, Chicago: University of Chicago Press.
Lakatos, I. and Musgrave, A. (eds.), (1971), *Criticism and the Growth of Knowledge*, Cambridge: Cambridge University Press.
Monod, J. (1972), transl. Wainhouse, A., *Chance and Necessity*, London: Collins.
O'Hear, A. (1980), *Karl Popper*, London: Routledge and Kegan Paul.
O'Hear, A. (1993), 'Historicism and Architectural Knowledge', *Philosophy 68*, 127–44.
Popper, K. (1950), 'Indeterminism in Quantum Physics and Classical Physics', *British Journal for the Philosophy of Science I*, 117–33, 173–95.
Popper, K. (1957), *The Poverty of Historicism*, London: Routledge and Kegan Paul.
Popper, K. (1959), *The Logic of Scientific Discovery*, London: Hutchinson (transl. of German ed., 1934).
Popper, K. (1963), *Conjectures and Refutations*, London: Routledge and Kegan Paul.
Popper, K. (1966), *The Open Society and Its Enemies* (5th ed.), 2 Vols., London: Routledge and Kegan Paul.
Popper, K. (1978), *Objective Knowledge* (2nd ed.), Oxford: Oxford University Press.
Popper, K. (1983), *Realism and the Aim of Science*, London: Hutchinson.
Popper, K. (1992), *Unended Quest: An Intellectual Autobiography* (revised ed.), London: Routledge.

Popper, K. (1997), ed. Bosetti, G., *The Lesson of the Century*, London: Routledge.

Popper, K. and Eccles, J. (1977), *The Self and Its Brain*, Berlin, Heidelberg, London, New York: Springer International.

Ruskin, J. (1985), ed. Wilmer, C., *Unto This Last and Other Writings*, Harmondsworth: Penguin Books.

Wallace, A. (1905), *My Life*, Vol. II, New York: Dodd, Mead.

Wittgenstein, L. (1961), transl. Pears, D. and McGuinness, B., *Tractatus Logico-Philosophicus*, London: Routledge and Kegan Paul.

Zerin, E. (1998), 'Karl Popper on God, the Lost Interview (1969)', *Skeptic 6*, no. 2, 47–8.

Acknowledgements

My fascination with the philosophy of Karl Popper began when I was a postgraduate at Warwick University. David Miller, Popper's former research assistant, joined the department and conducted a seminar series on *Conjectures and Refutations*. When I started my own university teaching career I continued working on Popper's thought, eventually producing my own study of his arguments in a book, which was published in 1980. I do not retract the detail of what I argued in that book, but more than 40 years later I do not feel that I did full justice to the depth and scope or indeed to the originality and independence of the vision which I now see underlay Popper's own philosophical career. In some small way I hope in this short book to rectify this deficiency in my earlier approach.

I met Popper himself only once, a memorable encounter shortly after my book had been published. In this encounter he revealed both the ferocity of his intellect, but also a genuine warmth to me and my efforts, which I deeply appreciated. While I saw no more of Popper himself, I kept in touch with David Miller, and I continued to discuss Popper's work with many other colleagues and friends, including some who had been personally close to Popper. So I would like here to record my gratitude for these discussions to John Watkins, Alan Musgrave, William Warren Bartley III, Tom Settle, Peter Munz, Bryan Magee, Antony Flew, Michael Redhead, Donald Gillies, Peter Clark, Elie Zahar, John Worrall, Colin Howson, Jeremy Shearmur, Larry Briskman, Hugh Mellor, Adolf Grünbaum, João Carlos Espada, Zuzana Párusnikova, Wenceslao Gonzales and Te Maire Tau. Te Maire helped me to see the relevance of Popper's thought to the situation in New Zealand when Popper lived there and subsequently. I also thank Charles Taliaferro warmly for urging me to write this book, and for invaluable suggestions.

History of Philosophy and Theology in the West

Alexander J. B. Hampton
University of Toronto

Alexander J. B. Hampton is a professor at the University of Toronto, specialising in metaphysics, poetics, and nature. His publications include *Romanticism and the Re-Invention of Modern Religion* (Cambridge 2019), *Christian Platonism: A History* (ed.) (Cambridge, 2021), and the *Cambridge Companion to Christianity and the Environment* (ed.) (Cambridge, 2022).

Editorial Board

Shaun Blanchard, *University of Notre Dame, Australia*
Jennifer Newsome Martin, *University of Notre Dame, USA*
Sean McGrath, *Memorial University*
Willemien Otten, *University of Chicago*
Catherine Pickstock, *University of Cambridge*
Jacob H. Sherman, *California Institute of Integral Studies*
Charles Taliaferro, *St. Olaf College*

About the Series

In the history of philosophy and theology, many figures and topics are considered in isolation from each other. This series aims to complicate this binary opposition, while covering the history of this complex conversation from antiquity to the present. It reconceptualizes traditional elements of the field, generating new and productive areas of historical enquiry, and advancing creative proposals based upon the recovery of these resources.

Cambridge Elements=

History of Philosophy and Theology in the West

Elements in the Series

The Metaphysics of Divine Participation
Alexander J. B. Hampton

C. S. Lewis on the Soul, God, and Christianity
Stewart Goetz

Popper, Philosophy and Faith
Anthony O'Hear

A full series listing is available at: www.cambridge.org/EHPT

For EU product safety concerns, contact us at Calle de José Abascal, 56–1°, 28003 Madrid, Spain or eugpsr@cambridge.org.

www.ingramcontent.com/pod-product-compliance
Ingram Content Group UK Ltd.
Pitfield, Milton Keynes, MK11 3LW, UK
UKHW021458220625
459949UK00018B/469